Business
Passport
to Japan

REVISED AND UPDATED EDITION

Business Passport to Japan

REVISED AND UPDATED EDITION

Sue Shinomiya and Brian Szepkouski

Stone Bridge Press • Berkeley, California

Published by
Stone Bridge Press
P. O. Box 8208
Berkeley, CA 94707
TEL 510-524-8732 • sbp@stonebridge.com • www.stonebridge.com

**For comments, questions, and suggestions, please contact
the authors at www.szepko-intl.com or +1 (908) 204-1221.**

Text © 2008 Sue Shinomiya and Brian Szepkouski.
Cover design by Linda Ronan.

Printed in the United States of America.

2011 2010 2009 2008 2007   10 9 8 7 6 5 4 3 2 1

LIBRARY OF CONGRESS CATALOGING-IN-PUBLICATION DATA
Shinomiya, Sue, 1961–
  Business passport to Japan / Sue Shinomiya and Brian Szepkouski.
— Rev. and updated ed.
      p. cm.
  ISBN 978-1-933330-47-1 (pbk.)
  1. Business etiquette—Japan. 2. Corporate culture—Japan. 3. Busi-
ness communication—Japan. 4. Japan—Commerce. I. Szepkouski,
Brian. II. Title.

HF5389.3.J3S55 2007
395.5'20952—dc22

                                    2007037544

Table of Contents

CHAPTER 2
Japan Overview 59

CHAPTER 3
Business in Japan 76

CHAPTER 4
Communication in Action 148

CHAPTER 5
Ten-Point Plan For Success 180

CHAPTER 6

Trends in a Global Japan *190*

CHAPTER 7

Beyond Survival: Exploring Japan *223*

CHAPTER 8

Useful Resources *241*

This book is dedicated to our respective children, Adam, and Hannah and Stephen, who are already mastering the art of bridging cultures—in their own special and unique ways.

Foreword

Welcome to the adventure of "mastering Japan" and to the updated and revised edition of our first book published in Japan five years ago. When we were approached by Stone Bridge Press, a U.S.-based publisher, it was an amazing second chance to perfect what we'd learned since our first edition. We still knew that dealing with Japan could be a daunting challenge. In a world made increasingly "flat" through technology, and with all the talk about BRIC (Brazil, Russia, India, and China), the temptation for businesspeople is to head straight for the mega-markets of China and/or India, with populations of over a billion each. Some might be wondering, "Is Japan still really worth the trouble?" But we discovered that the opposite was true: the interest in Japan has actually grown. Japan has begun to make a strong comeback from its decades-long economic slump and still remains vibrant as the world's second most important market, with the highest levels of innovation and technology, and among the highest levels of personal savings and household consumption. And at the same time, it has increasingly taken a role as the unofficial launching pad, or in their terms, "go-between," for doing business with the rest of Asia.

In late 2002 when *Business Passport to Japan* was released, we quickly realized that businesspeople were and still are hungry for user-friendly non-academic books that provide a real blueprint for success—and go into a little more detail than just a list of dos and don'ts. Globally, each of us has witnessed all things Japanese entering more aspects of our daily lives, from the Japanese electronics in our homes, to critically acclaimed movies and television shows alongside an increase in traditional Japanese imagery and Zen-like spirituality in interior design. Sushi has become the ubiquitous chic cuisine worldwide.

Since the release we have received numerous phone calls from all over the world, seen bookstores struggling to get more copies, and noticed universities adding our book to their textbook list. Some of our European clients were ecstatic to finally have a resource that explained Japan in clear terms, and others said it became their "bible" for establishing business in East Asia—some of whom are now managing multimillion-dollar businesses there! We were and are so grateful to play a role . . .

So now here it is: an updated and revised edition dedicated solely to the serious global businessperson, no matter where you are—Winnipeg, Johannesburg, Moscow, New York, Chennai, Sydney, and beyond!

This book is your guide to mastering a unique culture—one that has continually sought to add and borrow from other cultures, and then refine, shrink, and make more Japanese. Japan has always been curious about all other cultures and is invariably ready to integrate any ideas it deems worthy of importing. Japan can be intoxicating —its subtleties, beauty, and futuristic advancements have mystified people for centuries. It's a place where business rules, and where you may just find a gateway to China and the rest of Asia.

A quick housekeeping note on this edition: All Japanese names have been presented in Western order, that is, with family name last. Throughout, all Japanese words have been romanized in the Hepburn system.

We are pleased you have chosen this resource, and we hope that you will find your dealings with Japan rewarding and enriching in every sense.

Our aim has always been to allow our readers to walk away with a basic understanding of the secrets of doing business in Japan—to demystify some of those "non-tariff barriers" of culture and communication. Our own dealings with Japan span the last forty years, and we both continue to find it rewarding and enriching in every sense, professionally and personally. And we anticipate that anyone who picks up this book will too.

Wishing you continued success,

Sue Shinomiya
Portland, Oregon

Brian Szepkouski
Bernardsville, New Jersey

Acknowledgments

Our sincere gratitude goes to our project initiator and publisher of our first edition, Mr. Hiroshi Kagawa, and to Ms. Kyoko Kagawa for setting in motion the plans for this publication with Stone Bridge Press. We also appreciate the efforts of Stone Bridge Press, especially Mr. Peter Goodman for taking on this project and working with us so enthusiastically to ensure an even stronger second edition. Our thanks to Ms. Linda Ronan for her amazing technical production skill, Ms. Nina Wegner for her painstaking editing, and to Mr. Ari Messer, our publicist, for his creative ideas and energy.

We bow deeply to Ms. Ikuko Nagumo for her energy, input, and research, for setting up numerous appointments and interviews with her wide-ranging contacts in Japan, and for carefully checking through nearly every line of our manuscript.

The Honorable Shunji Yanai, former Japanese Ambassador to the U.S., deserves our appreciation for his articulation of the future vision for Japan. We also thank Mr. Masayuki Kohama for his insights on Japan's global business success, current business trends, and Japanese history.

Without a doubt, we are indebted to the many clients, associates, and friends who have provided words of wisdom, insights, valuable information, professional support, and relevant stories, many of which appear throughout this book: Mr. Shinichi Sato (United Airlines Cargo), Mr. Yuichiro Sato (Shimizu Corporation), Mr. Shigeru Itoh (Amistar Steel), Ms. Shinomiya's hundreds of clients and associates at Intel Japan, KK, Mr. Masahiko Konatsu (OAC), Mr. Chip Whitacre (Medtronic, Inc.), Mr. Yoshiyuki Mori (Merck & Co.), Dr. Kazunori Hirokawa (Daiichi-Sankyo), Mr. Toshiaki Hara (Johnson & Johnson), Ms. Yoshiko Fujinobe (Ryugaku Journal), Mr. Eisaku Yoshida (Merck & Co.), Mr. John Fuller (Kinokuniya New York), Ms. Noriko Ogami (Aperian Global, Japan), Mr. Vinay Chiniwar, the many managers and employees at Tektronix, Inc., the many employees of the Johnson & Johnson family of companies, Mr. Yamamoto of Seven-Eleven Japan, Dr. Ben Kedia (University of Memphis), Berlitz Cultural Consulting, Eisai Inc., Transnational Management Associates (TMA), Charis Intercultural Consulting, Mr. Clifford Clarke and all of our former associates of the Clarke Consulting Group, Portland State University's America Plus program and the dozens of participating university students from Japan and Asia, the Society of Intercultural Education, Training and Research (SIETAR) USA, and last but far from least, Mr. Takashi Shinomiya (Intel Corporation).

Our heartfelt thanks goes to family members and special friends who, in their own unique ways, motivated us to keep going, created the time and space for us to conduct research, travel, and basically complete the task of creating another book: Ms. Lori Halivopoulos, Ms. Joie Budington, Ms. Anne Szepkouski, Mr. Alex Szepkouski, members of the Bernardsville, New Jersey Rotary Club, Ms. Reiko Shinomiya, Ms. Patricia Kallenbach, and Dr. Warren Kallenbach.

And finally, we also acknowledge the friendship and professional association between these two authors, which has weathered not only two book editions, but also all the ups and downs of our past nearly three decades between the East Coast and West Coast, and between the U.S. and Japan.

Pre-quiz

Test Your Knowledge

This book is designed to be interactive, so we invite you to challenge yourself with our question-and-answer exercises, beginning with this pre-quiz. The purpose of this first quiz is to test your general knowledge of Japan. We would like to highlight the point that virtually any Japanese you meet could accurately answer similar questions about your country. This information would qualify as basic common sense, or *joshiki*, to most Japanese. So don't skip this part—it will provide some interesting insights into Japan today, and let you know where you are in terms of your *joshiki* about Japan. For those of you familiar with the previous edition of this book, check for new questions. Answers are at the back of this section. Have fun!

1 Name three famous Japanese people. (If you actually can, and two of them are not baseball stars, you are ahead of the game.)

2 Which of the following non-Japanese companies have done well in Japan?
McDonald's, Yahoo Japan, The Gap, Coca Cola, IBM, Intel, Apple, Motorola, Putnam Financial, Morgan Stanley, Microsoft, Mercedes Benz, BMW, Merrill Lynch, Citigroup, UBS, Procter & Gamble, Gillette, Aflac Insurance, General Electric, Hewlett Packard, Boeing, Johnson & Johnson, Pfizer, Coach, Inc., Louis Vuitton, Amway, Starbucks.

3 Approximately how long does it take to get from Narita International Airport to downtown Tokyo, and what's the taxi fare? Select one of the following (approx. ¥100 = US$1):
1) 1 hour / ¥5,000 (US$50)
2) 30 minutes / ¥3,500 (US$35)
3) 1.5 hours / ¥25,000 (US$250)
4) There are no taxis in Japan

4 Which is the worst faux pas?

1) In meetings: Falling asleep OR getting up and walking out in the middle?
2) At a restaurant: Sticking your chopsticks straight up into the rice OR pouring soy sauce onto your rice?
3) In resolving a customer conflict: Saying "No" directly to the customer OR asking a third party to get involved?

4) When building credibility with a business partner: Downplaying one's own accomplishments and being generally humble OR playing up the accomplishments of your Japanese partner?

 5 Who is Japan's biggest trading partner?

1) China
2) U.S.A.
3) Korea
4) Hong Kong
5) Germany
6) India

 6 What is Japan's favorite sport?

1) Sumo
2) Basketball
3) Soccer
4) Baseball
5) Karate

 7 Most Japanese homes have the following items:

1) Kimono for every member of the household
2) Slippers, usually two pairs or more, for every member of the household
3) A bidet-type toilet ("washlet")
4) A large-screen TV
5) A personal computer
6) HDTV (Called "Hi Vision")
7) A satellite dish
8) A high-tech rice cooker that talks
9) *Katana* swords

10) A special room for tea ceremony
11) A special room for bathing
12) A room with a straw mat floor
13) A special entryway area for taking off shoes
14) A shrine for praying to one's ancestors
15) A clothes washer and dryer
16) A balcony (whether it's the largest farmhouse or the tiniest apartment)
17) A microwave oven
18) A table with a built-in heating element underneath
19) Carpet with a heating element
20) At least one umbrella for every member of the household
21) A one-car garage
22) An automobile
23) A coffee maker
24) A bread maker
25) A picture of the current emperor
26) A lawn mower
27) A stone lantern
28) A pet
29) An Internet-accessible mobile phone that doubles as a camera and portable TV/video screen

8 What do Japanese identify as among the top problems in their society today?

1) Overcrowding
2) Pollution
3) Aging population
4) Health
5) Obesity and heart disease
6) High prices and inflation
7) Job security
8) Juvenile delinquency, underemployed youth

9) Economic recession

10) Kidnappings by North Korea

9 The local 7-Eleven or other convenience store is likely to . . . Check which ones apply:

1) Be located in a safe area, within a five-minute walk from your place of residence or hotel

2) Be clean, well lit, well laid out, fully staffed, and utilizing the most up-to-date inventory control systems in the world

3) Be a good place to pay your bills

4) Have an ATM at which you can open a bank account or add prepaid minutes to your cell phone

5) Be a good place to buy a fresh meal at any time of day or night

6) Have a wide selection of current magazines and even books

7) Have a copy machine and a fax machine in good working condition

8) Be a place where you can pick up and pay for your goods ordered by phone or Internet

9) Be a place from which you can send your suitcase to the airport, or other packages throughout Japan

10) Have more than ¥10,000 (US$100) in change in the register

10 Rank the following major cities in order of most to least expensive:

Tokyo, London, New York, Paris, Osaka, Copenhagen, Frankfurt, Zurich, Reykjavík.

11 Put a check next to the foods below that would be served at a typical restaurant in Japan:

1) Bulgoki

2) Tempura
3) Ramen
4) Sashimi
5) General Tsao's Chicken
6) Beef Satay
7) Chow mein
8) Curry rice
9) Dim sum

12 What are the top five leisure activities in Japan? Choose five from the following and rank them:

1) Golf
2) Skiing
3) Domestic travel (hot springs, etc.)
4) Watching videos
5) Driving
6) Special dining out
7) International travel
8) Watching sports events
9) Karaoke
10) Listening to music
11) Playing video games
12) Yoga and meditation

13 The annual household savings rate in Japan is:

1) Among the highest in the world
2) On par with the U.S.
3) Higher on a per household basis than China and Korea combined
4) Very low: Many Japanese households have huge credit card debts and mortgages due to the high cost of living

14 Which of the following are Japanese makers? Check all that apply:

1) Tata
2) Hyundai
3) Lenovo
4) Nokia
5) Honda
6) Samsung
7) Acer
8) Seiko
9) Canon
10) Nike
11) Sony

15 What major Japanese exports/trends/products have been making a splash around the world?

Answers to Quiz

1 Some possible answers: Ichiro Suzuki, Daisuke Matsuzaka (baseball players), Prince Shotoku, Emperor Hirohito, General Tojo, Ieyasu Tokugawa (historical figures), Junichiro Koizumi (Prime Minister 2001–6), Shinzo Abe (Prime Minister 2006–7), Yasuo Fukuda (Prime Minister 2007), Akio Morita (founder of Sony), Masayoshi Son (CEO of SoftBank, catalyst of Japan's Internet age), Katsuaki Watanabe (President and CEO of Toyota Motor), Satoru Iwata (CEO of Nintendo, in world's top thirty CEOs), Takafumi Horie (nationally popular Web entrepreneur, later convicted of securities fraud), Yasuhiro Nakasone (former Prime Minister), Sadako Ogata (former UN High Commissioner on Refugees), Princess Masako, Masaharu Morimoto (from *The Iron Chef*), Akira Kurosawa (filmmaker), Masi Oka (from U.S. TV show *Heroes*), Ken Watanabe (film actor), Hayao Miyazaki (animation filmmaker), Ryuichi Sakamoto (musician), Kitaro (musician), Seiji Ozawa (Boston Pops Conductor), Hanae Mori (designer), Lady Murasaki (author of *The Tale of Genji*), Shizuka Arakawa (2006 Olympic gold medalist skater), Mao Asada (skater), Kosuke Kitajima (2004 Olympic gold medalist swimmer), Shintaro Ishihara (governor of Tokyo, author of *The Japan That Can Say "No"*), Mari Matsunaga (woman who established the i-mode system for NTT DoCoMo), Shusaku Endo (writer), Beat Takeshi (comedian, actor, filmmaker), Hokusai (wood block print artist—"The Wave"), Taniguchi Yoshio (architect of The Museum of Modern Art, NYC), SMAP (hugely popular J-pop band, 1990s and 2000s).

> In written and spoken Japanese, the family name always comes before the given name.

2 All of them and many others. You can do well in Japan too.

3 About an hour and a half by limousine bus or car, if there's regular traffic, but it could take up to four hours. The taxi fare could run as high as ¥30,000 (about US$300).

4 1) Getting up and leaving in the middle (falling asleep might show your perseverance after working very hard).

2) Sticking your chopsticks straight up in rice (which is only done as an offering to the deceased at a funeral. Soy sauce on rice would just be considered odd).

3) Saying "No" directly to a customer (using a third party might help "save face").

4) Sorry, trick question. Both of these could help you build your credibility in relationships.

5 Until 2006, Japan's biggest trading partner was categorically the U.S. As of April 2007, China has surpassed the U.S. in terms of trade volume. The U.S.–Japan trade relationship is still one of the most important in the world. Trade with India is also on the rise.

6 Baseball, or *yakyu* as it's also known in Japan. Sumo remains quite popular but isn't enjoying the audiences it previously did. Soccer has gained popularity since Japan started the J-League, Japan's professional soccer league, and cohosted the World Cup in 2002.

7 The only items these authors have never seen in a Japanese home are the lawn mower and picture of the emperor. Rare: A kimono for every member of the household (too expensive), a special room for tea ceremony, *katana* swords, a one-car garage, large-screen TV (but these are becoming more popular), satellite dish, clothes dryer (most hang laundry out to dry), stone lantern (more commonly found in public gardens).

8 Note that overcrowding, pollution, obesity, and high prices are *not* really on the radar screen of current big issues. The others all could be identified as major issues, depending on what's getting media attention this week.

9 All apply.

10 Oslo, Paris, Copenhagen, London, Tokyo, Osaka, Reykjavík, Zurich, Frankfurt (The Economist Group 2007). Note that New York didn't even make the list this time thanks to fluctuations in the exchange rate.

11 1) Bulgoki (Wrong: Korean barbeque.)
2) Tempura (Correct: Interestingly enough, it was actually brought to Japan by the Portuguese.)
3) Ramen (Correct: Traditional noodle dish served in a flavorful broth; Chinese origin.)
4) Sashimi (Correct: Sliced raw fish. Combined with rice, it becomes sushi.)
5) General Tsao's Chicken (Wrong: Chinese-American dish.)

All "wrong" answers are actually eaten with great gusto in Japan at local Chinese, Thai, or Korean eateries.

6) Beef Satay (Wrong: Southeast Asian dish.)
7) Chow mein (Wrong: Chinese dish.)
8) Curry rice (Correct: Originally from India, but in Japan, it's more like the British version.)
9) Dim sum (Wrong: Chinese dish, called *yam cha* in Japanese.)

12 1) Special dining out 2) Domestic travel 3) Driving 4) Karaoke 5) Watching videos (*Japan Almanac 2006*)

13 Both 1) and 3) are correct. The savings rate in 2001 averaged about 10 percent of household income (compared to -1 percent in the U.S. in 2006), and total savings per household tops out at ¥12.7 million (US$110,000). That's a pretty good stash!

14 5) Honda 8) Seiko 9) Canon 11) Sony

15 Some key Japanese trends (for more on trends, see Chapter 6):

1) In Japan, aging population and lower birth rate leading to a decrease in population over time

2) Toyota edging out GM as #1 car manufacturer

3) Japanese cuisine, most notably sushi, becoming ubiquitous around the world—certification of authenticity, "bento" style lunch

4) Rise of Japanese pop culture worldwide, particularly in the form of *anime* (animation), horror films, video games, use of *kanji* as fashion motif (think tattoos), fashion for young people

5) Influence of Japanese traditional arts in home décor, landscaping, architecture, artwork, design

6) Baseball stars landing big contracts in the U.S. Major Leagues

7) Japanese retiring baby boomers spending their retirement bonuses

8) Lifestyle change in Japan: "Slow Life," people focusing more on leisure-time activities

9) Japanese individuals taking more risks with private investment and investing in overseas markets

10) Wireless applications via hand-held devices—Japan leads the way in mobile phone innovation, features

11) Continuing to push the envelope of quality—Japan is the still the global benchmark

Wrap Up

So how did you do? If you got even a few of these answers, your knowledge of Japan is better than most. Now you're ready to launch preparations for Japan.

(Source for questions 12, 13, and 15: *Asahi Shimbun's Japan Almanac 2006*)

Introduction

So maybe you're on the plane to Japan right now, even as you are reading this. Well, we're very glad you are reading this now and not after your visit. When you get off the plane at Narita, your journey is just beginning. After the long walk down several corridors and through quarantine (What was that?), you see the lines at immigration for returning Japanese, which are moving quickly and effortlessly. Then you follow the non-Japanese crowds to the long, snail-paced lines for non-Japanese. You realize you haven't filled out the immigration forms. In your jet-lagged state, it's about all you can do to stand for another fifteen minutes. When was the last time you used the word "embarkation"—English here may be different. Finally at the counter, the stone-faced immigration official looks you over, but you make it through! You follow the crowds again down the escalator to get your luggage off the carousel. Someone races ahead of you to get a luggage cart, another one pushes you aside just as you reach for your bag, then someone else cuts in front of you in line for customs inspection. Whatever happened to the polite Japanese you were told about? And what's with the wide array of get-ups young people are sporting, from mod to grunge? No kimonos? No, not here!

You go through customs, happy about the gracious treatment you receive there. You might be wondering why no one even looked at your suitcase—or maybe they picked through everything. You come out through the sliding doors and, in your jet-lagged state, vaguely hope someone will be holding a placard with your name on it. But everything you see is in Japanese. You knew that would be the case, but when it actually happens it's almost overwhelming. You need help, and the signs aren't very helpful.

Let's see, you need money. Is this an ATM? No, it appears to dispense only telephone cards. Now, how are they used? Interesting that every phone in the airport has an ISDN (Integrated Services Digital Network) port but nobody is using them. In fact, nobody seems to be using payphones much at all but rather their sleek, multi-functional mobile phones. And what's with all the bling dangling off the sides of the phones? Ahhh, you spy a Citibank ATM. Maybe you can actually get cash out of this in yen. Little do you suspect that some ATMs stop dispensing cash at 6:00 p.m. and that might be the last Citibank machine you'll see for a few days. You spy a plethora of counters advertising mobile phones for rent— but which to choose? You wander around for a while, bumping into people who seem to want to pass on the left, and you wonder how you are supposed to get to your hotel. Taxi? Got about $250 to spare?

Stop! Go back. Start over again. Nobody prepared me for *this* Japan.

Don't panic. Even the most seasoned veterans who've done business in Japan successfully for years will tell you it's *still* just about the most challenging business environment on earth.

You have probably been asked by your company to accomplish a particular goal vis à vis Japan. Going back to Atlanta or Zürich and telling your company that you've mastered the subway system won't impress anyone back at the home office, even though that may have been quite a challenging barrier on the ground in Japan. Achieving your objectives will impress them, and that's what this book is about. Why not make it easier on yourself?

Through the years, we've dealt with many who were unable to complete their stated goals. We've consulted for people who had made the trip to Japan and botched the negotiations with the result that they had to backtrack and mend fatally damaged relationships. That costs weeks if not months and potentially thousands of dollars or euros. We've spent years in Japan on the receiving end of failed customer negotiations that might have been headed off with just a few quick upfront tips. Many of the themes we covered in our first book are still relevant, and even more so as the economy in Japan is finally back on the move, and moving quickly in new directions.

Opportunities in Japan

We all understand that Japan is still holding its own as the second-largest economy in the world—there is money to be made there. The question is, how? The quick-fix scheme won't work. Yet, the business opportunities there are abundant. Japan has the most sophisticated, affluent consumers on the planet. How to reach them? Japan is not easy to navigate and horror stories are plentiful. Indeed, many believe Japan is too complicated, with too many barriers—logistical, linguistic, regulatory, cultural—to succeed there. Certainly, you don't want to be like Sisyphus ceaselessly pushing the rock uphill, when a few tools will ease the struggle. We believe that business in Japan does not have to be a Sisyphean ordeal. This book is designed to be a tool for your success.

About This Book

Among the many "how to" books on business in Japan, few provide a user-friendly, strategic blueprint for business success targeted at the global business traveler in the twenty-first century.

An effective blueprint for success in Japan should include the following:

- How business is conducted in Japan: business protocol, strategies, communication style.
- Cultural and historical influences on business.
- Specific tips on what to do and what not to do.
- How to get around in Japan logistically, including information on transportation and food.
- How to make the most of your visit, including your precious down time.
- How to design an approach to building enduring professional and personal relationships.
- Specific tips for women doing business in Japan.

The format is designed to be challenging, inter-active, and fun to read. We hope you will take away a basic understanding of how business gets done in Japan, whether you invest five minutes reading the now stream-lined Ten-Point Plan for Success in Chapter 5, or the few hours it takes to read the entire book. In short, we hope this book will be a springboard for the start of your career working with Japan, and, for seasoned Japan hands, we hope to provide some refreshing new perspectives on the issues you've been dealing with for years, plus updated information including statistics and anecdotes that reflect current changes in Japan, which we hope will endure for years to come.

Go back through the Table of Contents—there might be sections you need more immediately than oth-ers. As your business trip progresses, new questions are likely to pop up. The book can be approached from any angle, in any order, as needed. We suggest you keep it with you on your trip. You might regard it as one of your essential travel documents. Good luck!

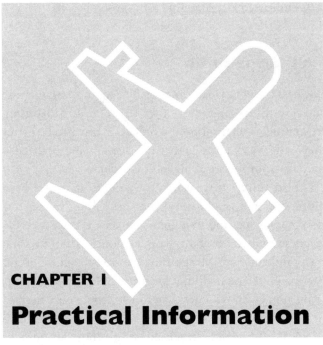

CHAPTER 1

Practical Information

Here are some typical questions about practical matters that businesspeople bound for Japan ask in our consulting and training practices:

1. Do I need a visa?
2. How much is the taxi fare from the airport?
3. Do I really need to bring a suit? Is it true that Japanese women never wear pantsuits?
4. Can I plug my computer into the wall, and can I use my mobile phone there?
5. How many business cards do I need to bring, and do they really need to be printed in Japanese?
6. Do I need an interpreter?
7. How long is the flight?
8. What happens if I can't eat the food? And what if I can't use chopsticks?

9. Do I need to bring gifts for everybody?

Preparing to Go

Business travel in Japan can be a challenging, stimulating, and rewarding experience. It can also be an exhausting, frustrating, even disorienting ordeal. In order to be better prepared, we've put together this section and updated it to make your logistical life a little easier.

First thing's first: When traveling to Japan for brief visits, you will need a valid passport through the duration of your stay and six months beyond. Check with the Japanese Embassy or local consulate for the latest visa and travel information. Most business travelers coming to Japan for short visits will not need a visa. However, if your sojourn in Japan is longer than ninety days, you will need to secure a valid work visa.

Set your agenda in advance with those whom you will be meeting in Japan. Have they confirmed this agenda with you? Is it too ambitious? Have you built in any time for relationship-building, relaxing, sightseeing, shopping, and/or time to yourself?

Make sure that all hotels have been reserved. It is generally best to stay near the area where you'll do business. This will reduce the uncertainty when considering the time necessary to go from point A to point B, especially the possibility of your taxi getting stuck in traffic or of your misreading subway or train maps and time schedules. Get input from your Japanese counterparts. They should have the perfect recommendation on where to stay (most likely where they have a corporate rate), and they might even kindly make the reservation for you. These days you might be able to find a better hotel rate on the

Internet or via your hotel's Web site, which will also give you a better sense of where you will be staying.

Read up on Japan. You're doing that right now. Consider looking at other books and even Web sites, some of which are listed in Chapter 8 in this book. Just to check your understanding of the country, have fun with the pre-quiz (see page 15) if you haven't already. What amazes most international business people, once they're in Japan, is how much Japanese know about people from other countries and how little we seem to know of them. This can be a very eye-opening experience. It's always best to arrive with some knowledge of Japan and what's in store for you.

Use your preparation stage as an opportunity to develop relationships with your Japanese counterparts. Let them help prepare you for what to expect especially on the business end. This will be covered more specifically in Chapter 3, "Business in Japan," but here are a few tips. Speak slowly and deliberately, especially on the telephone. If you're communicating by e-mail, try to keep your messages simple and confined to one or two points only. Have patience with their English and let them finish their sentences. Try to be accommodating and show appreciation for the smallest favors. The more you can do to lay the interpersonal groundwork, the easier it will be to conduct your business dealings after you arrive.

Jet Lag

Jet lag is a hard reality on trips to Japan—especially for those arriving from Europe and the Americas. Flights from these regions to Japan are quite long, about fourteen hours direct from New York. Once in Japan, it could take as much as a week to fully conquer jet lag.

The most tried-and-true method of seasoned travelers is to stay awake as long as possible on the day you arrive, until, say, 11 p.m., then sleep until at least 7 a.m. to take on the local sleeping schedule as soon as possible. To further ease the effects of jet lag, some travelers take Melatonin, a dietary supplement, to induce sleep. For anything stronger, it is advisable to check with your physician first. Alcohol can either help or exacerbate your time adjustment. But don't punish yourself over jet lag. You will not be alone in your grogginess. And often more severe is the jet lag upon return home—be cautious about scheduling meetings on the day of your return.

Numbers: Superstition Taken Seriously

Japanese generally give gifts in sets of "lucky" numbers, generally numbers that cannot be divided, such as three, five, and seven, but also eight or nine. The number four (*shi*) is a synonym for death, so its use is avoided in many instances such as in addresses and product names. Some hotels still don't offer any fourth-floor rooms. A famous European tennis-ball manufacturer wasn't successful in Japan until they stopped selling in sets of four—three to a can is the standard. One U.S. businessperson told us about a project he'd worked on in Japan that had a phase one, phase two, and phase three, then suddenly the sequencing changed to "Phase 3.1" for no apparent reason. When in doubt, ask your Japanese colleagues.

Packing

When packing, think light. Remember that there will be lots of walking and stairs and huge numbers of people bumping into you in airports and train stations. Only bring luggage with wheels to save the strain on your muscles. It is surprising that there are often no elevators or escalators in even the busiest train stations or other public places. In countries like Japan where you're likely to use a range of transport, it's difficult to maneuver with large heavy bags. Ask your hotel to hold larger bags for you if you're taking a short trip and coming back.

Come Bearing Gifts

Japanese love to give and receive gifts; some amount of preparation on your part, therefore, will be appreciated. Consider bringing corporate gifts such as pens or polo shirts with logos, neatly wrapped for the people you will be meeting. If you will be interacting with a large group, bring something to share, such as a box of high-quality chocolates or other local sweets. Just give it to one of the Japanese staff members to set out for the group to enjoy with tea or coffee. For business travelers returning to Japan to meet with individual colleagues whom you have come to know well, consider bringing more personal items, such as small-sized perfume samplers, fine towels, wine, whiskey, or golf balls. If you know their family, you can bring toys, etc. for the kids. It doesn't hurt to ask "What can I get you from the U.S.?" Note that presentation is exceedingly important—gifts need to be wrapped—and items should be checked to assure that gifts were not manufactured or assembled in Japan or places nearby like China or Southeast Asia. We recommend reading the section on gift giving in Chapter 3.

Wardrobe

Compared to the U.S., dress in Japan tends to be far more formal; men wear suits and ties more often, not only to work, but also to various social events. The company uniform might be less ubiquitous than previously, but you will still see many of these, particularly in manufacturing. Casual dress in the workplace is not as widespread as in the rest of the world, though high-tech and other trend-oriented industries in Japan are becoming more business casual. Don't forget to pack slip-on shoes since you will be taking off your shoes whenever stepping onto a *tatami* mat, entering someone's home, or entering some offices and research centers. If you bring lace-up shoes, you will fall well behind the rest of your group whenever leaving or entering various establishments. Also bring new or really good socks or stockings so that you can avoid the embarrassment of having your big toe sticking out for all to see. For men, white or light blue shirts with conservative ties still dominate the business scene. "Cool Biz" may be a trend word, but not a good choice if you want to be taken seriously.

Women and Pantsuits

Conventional wisdom for women in Japan follows a conservative approach to attire—dark suit, white or light-colored blouse, conservative pumps. Recently, however, greater variety for women in the workplace, particularly in high-tech industries, has become common. Pantsuits are quite acceptable. They are in fact highly recommended, because they make it easier to sit on the floor—which you likely will be doing at some point—than in a tight skirt. Loose, longish skirts with a suit jacket also work well and allow for more outfit options. Even though some of the younger Japanese women might be wearing short skirts, they can be awkward when removing shoes or sitting on the floor in a high-class Japanese restaurant. Go lightly on the jewelry and perfume. It is especially important for women to convey professionalism at all times. Attention to detail will not go unnoticed. Your image may depend more on what you wear and how you carry yourself than it does in Western countries.

Diversity Acceptance

Given our increasingly diverse global work environments, you may be wondering how Japan handles traditionally underrepresented individuals, especially those coming from the U.S. or Europe. In Japan the diversity categories basically boil down to this: you are either Japanese or not Japanese. The population is 99 percent ethnically Japanese. Becoming a Japanese citizen is not a birthright—even in a family that has lived in Japan for several generations, one must adopt a Japanese name and go through a rigorous process to gain citizenship. So when in Japan, you will first and foremost be seen as a foreigner, or *gaijin*. Your skin color, gender, sexual orientation, or religion is secondary. Unless you happen to be ethnically Japanese, most Japanese will assume that as an outsider you are unfamiliar with Japanese language, customs, and ways. Once you get past the barrier of being a foreigner and the possible barrage of questions around being different, you may experience a range of reactions, from being treated as an instant celebrity, to being marginalized as an outsider, to possibly over time being "just another (foreign) member of the team."

In some ways, the playing field is more level for non-Japanese because they are "outside of the system" to begin with. For example, we've known many women and people of color who struggled with historical underrepresentation in business in their own countries, but became extremely successful in Japan. Anyone can succeed with the right amount of effort, patience, and willingness to adjust.

Not Traveling Alone?

Unless your spouse, significant other, or relative has

specifically been invited on your Japan trip, be sure to consider the logistical challenges first before setting out together. You will very likely not be spending much time together. In Japan the separation of family and work is clearly defined. On dinners out, golf outings, or even sightseeing trips it's unlikely that you will find Japanese accompanied by their significant others, even if they work for the same company. This is not only culturally appropriate, but also mutually agreeable for the spouses. Your counterparts may or may not object to your bringing someone along, but they will probably be uncomfortable with the notion.

Our Essential Japan-Bound Checklist

- Passport and travel documents: You'd be surprised how easy it is to forget these items.
- Money: Take an alternate credit card as it's possible yours will be "rejected" for no apparent reason. Sometimes your credit card company will kick in the fraud protection if charges are made abroad. Carry cash!
- Computer equipment: Your laptop should work fine, but check your plug adapter.
- Internet access: Most hotels have wireless or cable access, but you may have to rely on the biz center of your hotel for some tasks.
- Plug adapter: Your electrical equipment might not work in Japanese plugs.
- Camera: Commemorative photos will be appreciated. It's very easy to make prints from digital cameras anywhere in Japan.
- Map of Tokyo or other areas you'll travel to: See our abbreviated version on page 253. Free bilingual maps can be obtained from the Japan

National Tourist Organization desk at the international airports in Japan.

- Gifts/presents: For more information, see Chapter 3.

- Handkerchiefs or small tissue packet: Many restrooms don't have paper towels. Some have elaborate bidet functions and toilet seat sanitiz-ers, but no paper towels.

- Business cards: Bring at least three times more than you think you might need; it is bad form to run out. Rule of thumb: take about a hundred for a week-long trip.

- A proper business card holder: This is an es-sential item in the land of the business card ex-change ritual. See Chapter 3.

Don't bother with:

- Spare toothbrushes, hair brushes, combs, shav-ing cream, razors, hair dryers, shampoo, condi-tioner, and slippers—most hotels will supply you with these as part of the service of a good hotel.

What's More Expensive in Japan?

- Gasoline: The price is about two times higher than in the U.S. This affects the price of virtu-ally everything else.

- Trains: Bullet trains are especially expensive. A trip from Tokyo to Osaka costs about the same as a plane ticket.

- Beverages: In a swank hotel, a soft drink or cof-fee drink can cost as much as ¥1,800 (US$18). You are paying for using the space and partaking of the ambiance more than for the beverage.

- Rental Cars: Cars cost as much as ¥20,000 (US$200) a day for an ordinary car.
- Road Tolls: A long jaunt to the countryside might cost as much as ¥30,000 (US$300).

What about the Food?

You may have heard that the food is exotic, but you can rest assured that there are plenty of familiar things to eat. Japanese cuisine is not limited to raw fish and tofu. Certainly, there is all manner of fish but also beef, pork, chicken, ham, bacon, vegetables, noodles, breads, fruit, and more. In the cities, one can find restaurants featuring virtually any of the world's fine cuisines. Don't go without trying the different kinds of noodles: *ramen* (long thin wheat noodles), *soba* (buckwheat noodles), *udon* (larger, thick wheat noodles), and *somen* (vermicelli–like wheat noodles). Most foreigners find these dishes fun and delicious.

Another Fast Food Nation?
On his first visit to the U.S. last year, one ten-year-old Japanese friend of the author's family remarked his astonishment: "Gee, I was surprised that they have McDonald's here too!" Surely this is testimony to Japan's still amazing ability to take an impossibly alien concept and somehow refine it and make it completely indigenous.

If you have any strong aversions toward any type of food, health considerations, or religious preferences, just let your counterparts know in advance so that neither you nor they will be in an awkward position. The real frustration is in not knowing what is in certain foods. Whenever possible, discreetly try to check with someone who can identify the ingredients for you. Most visitors to Japan are pleasantly surprised about the incredible variety of food and delicate flavoring.

GENERAL TIP: Menu items that end in or start with "*yaki*" are cooked, easy to eat, and tasty. For example, *yaki tori* (grilled chicken on a skewer), *yaki zakana* (grilled fish), *teppan yaki* (like Benihana's but without the chef's showoff moves—an American invention), and *sukiyaki* (beef and vegetables cooked in a shallow pot at the table). If you happen to be keen on beef, try Kobe beef, which many will argue is the best beef in the world. In the end, whether you're vegan, kosher, halal, or just plain finicky, Japanese cuisine has something for everyone.

For survival eating, you can always frequent familiar haunts such as McDonald's, KFC, Denny's, Wendy's, Pizza Hut, Starbucks, Mister Donut, or coming soon: Burger King. Note of caution: Watch out for localization of food items. That chocolate cream-filled doughnut you thought you ordered might actually be filled with sweet bean paste. It's probably better for you anyway. The pizza will be very familiar, but for variety you could try the tuna or even squid toppings. For other fast food, or for the fun of it, you might also try Mos Burger or Freshness Burger—the names may sound less than appetizing, but they both offer healthful fare, including rice burgers, with rice-cake buns instead of bread buns. If your preference runs to nutrition bars or vitamin drinks, any local 7-Eleven or other convenience store can satisfy that and most other cravings at virtually any hour. Check out, for example, the *onigiri* (rice balls wrapped in seaweed, containing any variety of fillings) and the way they are carefully wrapped in cellophane. A perennial favorite is the tuna salad roll (the canned variety, with mayonnaise). You can also get grilled salmon or chicken, usually over rice, or noodles that are a breeze to prepare. You might find fresh salads ranging from green to creamy potato to macaroni

1
2
3
4
5
6
7
8

vegetable dishes, a variety of yogurts, as well as the usual range of junk food snacks. Or how about trying *nikuman*, tasty steamed buns with seasoned pork or other filling?

Upon Arrival

Immigration, Currency, Tipping

When landing at either Narita (formerly known as the New Tokyo International Airport) or Kansai International (near Osaka; Kansai refers to the region where Osaka is located), you will quickly note how clean everything is. Narita has been remodeled as a state-of-the-art facility, while Kansai is a newer airport, splendidly designed by the noted Italian architect Renzo Piano. Notice the artwork suspended from the ceiling.

After clearing immigration, you will proceed to the baggage-claim area. Airlines and flights are clearly marked. Baggage handling in Japan is done efficiently and bags usually arrive promptly. At some domestic airports you may even find your luggage already waiting for you as you enter the baggage-claim area. Moreover, you don't have to stress out about watching your bags. Petty theft (in fact, all crime) in Japan is very low.

Clearing customs in Japan is generally painless, requiring that one merely respond to a couple of pro forma questions, such as "What is the purpose of your visit?" "Do you have anything to declare?" "What is in your bag?" or "How long will you stay in Japan?" The next step is to exchange money, which can do either inside the customs hall or just outside, or you can go to the nearest compatible ATM. All currency exchange counters and banks in the airports in Japan offer pretty much the same rate, generally better than the rate at your hotel. If you need assistance, go to the Information Counter where you can use English. And don't forget, Japanese drive on the left side of the road, so they are inclined to walk past you on the left also.

In the past, Japan has been primarily a cash-based society. Most people have credit cards, but they are not used as often as in Western countries. Your bankcard may or may not work in a lot of ATMs in Japan. Most people carry around ¥30,000–¥50,000 in cash (US$300–$500).

You will not need any money for tipping. This practice does not exist in Japan. No need to tip anybody for any reason. Service people earn living wages, and excellent service is a matter of course. In fact, some service personnel, such as bellhops, might even be embarrassed when denying your offer.

Getting into Tokyo

Japan has perhaps the most advanced transportation system of any industrialized country in the world, running the gamut from high-speed bullet trains to typical one-speed bicycles carrying mom, the groceries, and often two kids all at once—with no helmets. Sample as many modes of transport as your time in Japan allows. Well, maybe not the bikes with the whole family, but first here's how to get from the airport to Tokyo.

There are several choices: taxi, limousine bus, Narita Express (a train, known as N'EX), and the Keisei Skyliner (train bound for Ueno Station). Taxis can cost anywhere from ¥20,000–¥30,000, a stretch for most people. All other public transportation into downtown Tokyo is roughly ¥3,000. If your final destination is a city other than downtown Tokyo, check with the information counter about air connections—you might need to change terminals—or about direct buses or trains. There's a new line connecting Narita and Haneda Airports called the Keihin Kyuko. Here are the choices for getting into Tokyo in more detail:

Taxi

ADVANTAGES

- The most convenient way to get right to the door of your destination, especially if you have more than one person along and a lot to carry.
- It's easy to catch a taxi, generally within a minute, whether at the airport or in the city.
- Clean, safe service and a pleasant experience.
- You never have to open or close a taxi door—it's operated automatically by the driver.

DISADVANTAGES

- Quite expensive (see above)—the fare will start at ¥660 (about US$6), but goes up after 11 p.m. Again, no tipping required.
- Subject to unpredictable traffic patterns, even if your destination is relatively close.
- If it's not a major destination, you'll need to be able to explain where you're going: be sure to have the address and directions written out with a map or have a native Japanese explain your destination to the driver.
- Most have navigation sytems—a few don't though, so you could have problems if they don't know your destination.
- Accidentally closing or opening the taxi door yourself could result in your being soundly scolded by the driver.

Limousine Bus

This is probably the best choice for most. Look for the well-marked orange-colored counters in the arrival lobby.

Advantages

- It's easy to figure out your destination; the bus drops you at the Tokyo City Air Terminal (T-CAT) or at your hotel. It stops at virtually all major hotels and train stations in Tokyo.
- It's easy to figure out how to pay.
- Stops right outside the airport arrival lobby.
- No hassling with carrying your own bags.

Disadvantages

- For people with long legs, it may feel cramped.
- Traffic jams can cause all kinds of delays and a less predictable arrival time. Trips can take approximately one and a half to as much as four hours, depending on traffic.
- No food/drinks sold on board. OK to bring your own.
- No smoking on the bus.
- Buses usually have a lavatory on board, but not always.

N'EX (Narita Express, direct train to the center of Tokyo)

Go down the escalator in the arrival lobby.

Advantages

- Fastest service to downtown Tokyo—approximately sixty minutes, and you will arrive on time.
- Departures are usually scheduled every half hour.
- Trains are generally spacious.
- Reserved seating.

- Smooth ride.
- Plenty of restrooms.
- Smoking cars.
- Good connection if going on to Yokohama.
- Food and beverages are sold on board.

DISADVANTAGES

- Requires reservation, but can be made on the spot.
- Some trains are sold out, requiring a considerable wait for the next train with an open seat.
- First-time visitors may have difficulty figuring out payment and final destination.

Keisei Skyliner (direct train to Ueno Station in the East Center of Tokyo)

Go down the escalator in the arrival lobby.

ADVANTAGES

- More departures than N'EX.
- Faster than the bus, no traffic delays.
- Comfort level almost the same as N'EX.
- A little cheaper than N'EX.

DISADVANTAGES

- Similar to N'EX—also not as convenient for many Tokyo destinations.

Getting into Osaka

For those arriving at Kansai International, you can take the Haruka (to Shin Osaka Station), which takes about forty-five minutes, or Rapito Nankai Railway to Namba terminal, which is located in the central downtown area of Osaka. Cost is approximately ¥1,500 and it takes about thirty minutes.

Post–arrival in Japan

Public Transportation in Japan

Trains and buses strictly follow set schedules, which are posted and easy to read. Some five million people commute in and around Tokyo an average of an hour and a half a day. This accounts, by the way, for the proliferation of such products as personal stereos and even TVs, books that are small and light weight, adult comic books, and Internet-capable mobile phones from which you can check Web sites, send text messages to your friends or work associates, download books and even video content, or more recently, watch TV programs. The mass-commuting phenomenon is not lost on advertisers, who spend liberally on well-placed print ads and flat panel moving-screen ads decorating the insides of all trains. Several million captive eyeballs for several hours every day! Jackpot!

If you find yourself away from metropolitan areas, not every station has signs in English. You may want to study the Japanese characters, or *kanji*, for your destination station, so that you will be able to recognize them. If you get lost, ask someone for help. This is a situation in which Japanese, wanting to be good hosts, will usually very willingly help a total stranger.

Subways and Trains

Give them a try. Here the some pros and cons:

PROS

- Many convenient lines, especially in major cities.
- If you miss one, another will come in just a few minutes.
- Good connections.

- Not subject to traffic jams—a big plus.
- Safe, clean, well lit, convenient kiosks, color coded.
- Clearly marked signs are mostly bilingual, especially in major cities.
- Generally quieter than any other trains you've been on, even at rush hour.

Cons

- Stairs to climb, and lots of them. They are shallow, so watch your footing and travel lighter than usual.
- Not all trains announce destinations in English.
- Some rush-hour trains are so packed that they can be difficult to get on and uncomfortable to ride (unless you would like to have the visceral experience of the proverbial sardine).
- Riding the trains after 10 p.m. or so, you could find yourself uncomfortably close to an overly inebriated person. In rare cases, this could result in a redecoration of your wardrobe.

Tips for Train Travel

- If you can't figure out the fare from the map above the ticket vending machine, take the lowest fare option. When you get off the train, proceed to either the "Fare Adjustment" machine, or the ticket window near the exit.
- As mentioned previously, don't be surprised if some kind Japanese person offers to help you figure out your destination and fare. Japanese will often help strangers find their way.
- Save your ticket after boarding the train—you'll need it again at the end of the ride.

- Note that people don't usually eat on the subway or train, unless it's a long-distance trip.

Bullet Trains or *Shinkansen*

A bullet train offers a smooth ride and is unbelievably fast. It's only fifteen minutes by *Shinkansen* (bullet train) from Tokyo to Yokohama and about two-and-a-half hours to Osaka (a distance of 360 miles). There are reserved and non-reserved seats. If you really want space and comfort, try the Green Car for a few thousand yen more. The trains feature every sort of amenity. Restrooms are available in every other car. You'll also find payphones. Note that when using cell phones, passengers are expected to go to the space between the cars, called the deck, to hold conversations. Attendants roam the cars with a wide array of items to eat and drink—provided you are prepared to pay about double the normal rate.

The *Shinkansen* is probably the best way to travel between Tokyo and Osaka. While flying is faster from airport to airport, the *Shinkansen* stops in the centers of both cities and renders the time-consuming transfers at the airports unnecessary.

Communication Essentials

Using the Telephone

Many hotels offer discount rates on international calls. Local calls are generally ¥10 or less for every three minutes. The most convenient way to use public phones is with a prepaid phone card, though of course you can use coins for most phones. In most cases, calling internationally is much cheaper using your hotel phone or a payphone than it will be from your rental mobile phone.

Phone card dispensers can usually be found near any bank of public phones or at train station kiosks. Standard price for a phone card is ¥1,000. Insert your card, making sure the arrow or triangle is pointing toward the phone. The digital display (many phones have the option of a digital display in English) will register how many units you have on your card. Enter the phone number. As you talk, the display will register the dwindling units as they are used up. If your units expire during a call, the phone will spit your card out and you will have only a very few seconds left to complete the call before being cut off. If you have another card, you can insert it at this time, and continue your call as needed.

It's an irony that many phones in Japan were outfitted to handle ISDN (computer modem) lines before the current wireless phone boom, rendering the ISDN jack all but useless. Even payphones are becoming harder to find.

Mobile Phones (*Keitai Denwa*)

Wireless technology is more advanced in Japan than most other countries and cell phones are everywhere. People simply don't leave home without them, and people frequently upgrade to the latest model. Don't assume your mobile phone, even if it's "global," will operate in Japan. Japan, as usual, is the exception. You can rent or buy a mobile phone and install your SIM card. The problem is that roaming charges are exorbitant, and you will be charged the highest rates. Better to rent a phone with a local phone number, or purchase a prepaid cell phone. You can rent a cell phone on a day-to-day basis in Japan, as we mentioned earlier, from one of the many counters at the airport upon arrival. As of 2007, at least a dozen companies offer rental mobile phones at the airport. Typical rates as of 2007 were around ¥1,000 (US$10) per week plus ¥250–¥1,000 per day, and ¥75 per minute of airtime. A drawback is that the functions will be different and could be harder to understand, plus display info for Internet connectivity and e-mail may not be in English, and Internet access could use up your prepaid minutes really fast. Fortunately, numbers are universal. Your hotel concierge might also be able to arrange a phone for you, at a price of course. When you return your mobile phone at the airport, go to the same counter you rented from (if you can remember which one), and don't assume they will give you a receipt right away. The process is a bit confusing.

Getting Connected: E-mail and More

You can plug in and get online just about anywhere in Japan. Wireless networks abound, although most of them are geared for mobile phones. Check with your hotel about how to connect to their wireless or cable system. There are also many Internet spaces; some come complete with your own cubicle that can be rented by the hour. Japan leads the world in cutting-edge fiber optic connections, so you should have no trouble getting online.

How to Communicate Even If You Don't Speak Japanese

The bad news: It is unlikely that you will gradually just pick up Japanese off the street, even if that is how you learned your Spanish in Mexico. In fact, some people who have lived in Japan for decades can barely carry on a conversation. The good news: These same people not only manage but are thriving. It's really not so much a matter of mastering the language but rather finessing the culture and understanding how to communicate "better" in English. That's right. You can communicate in English. It just has to be a version that is understandable for people who may have learned English to prepare them for an entrance exam. Here are some pointers to ease the communication gap:

- Speak slowly and deliberately. This request has been made over and over again by Japanese who work with English speakers.
- Use simpler words and sentence structures—avoid slang and complex vocabulary.
- Don't speak louder, speak more gently. Allow plenty of pause time after questions and between sentences.
- Try to "chunk" your thoughts—so you don't end up using really long sentences.
- When you are not understood, try saying the exact same sentence again (don't paraphrase).
- If all else fails, try writing it down. Japanese often read better than they speak.
- Learn basic Japanese pronunciation. If you can pronounce certain vocabulary items as a Japanese would, you can increase your chances of being understood.

These strategies and more will be explained in detail in the business chapters later in this book.

Survival Phrases

Feel free to learn and use the following phrases. Check the guide on the next page for correct pronunciation; if your pronunciation is off, you might not be understood. Don't worry if your listener answers you in English. It's only to make you feel more comfortable. If you say one word in Japanese, your hosts will no doubt be quite pleased and shower you with praise on your "perfect Japanese." A completely bilingual person, on the other hand, is much more likely to be criticized and corrected for his or her errors. What's especially important is pronouncing names correctly. Many of our clients have actually found that spoken Japanese is easier to learn than they had originally thought. We encourage you to give it a try.

Fundamentals for Pronouncing Japanese

1. Vowel Sounds: There are five vowels in Japanese, and they are always pronounced the same way. They are essentially the same vowel sounds found in Spanish and Italian:

a	–	ah as in "ah"
i	–	ee as in "we"
u	–	oo as in "soon"
e	–	eh as in "get"
o	–	oh as in "old"

   If you're having trouble remembering the sounds, try this handy mnemonic device: "Ah we soon get old," which captures each vowel sound in order (and which is what you might be feeling, considering the time it takes to learn even a few phrases of Japanese).

2. Japanese "r": The "r" sound in Japanese combines "l" and "r." The tongue hits the roof of the mouth, similar to the "r" in Spanish, but without the trill.

3. Stress and Accent: Unlike other languages where stress and accent play an important role (for example, English generally accents the penultimate syllable of a word), Japanese is best spoken almost in a monotone voice.

Basic Phrase List

Greetings

- *Hajimemashite* → Nice to meet you. (Literally "It's the first time.")
- *Ohayo gozaimasu* → Good morning. (At the end of a word, the "u" in "su" is usually dropped.)
- *Konnichi wa* → Hello. (11:30 a.m. to sundown.)
- *Moshi moshi* → Hello. (Used only over the phone.)

All-Purpose Phrases

- *Domo* → Thanks. (Casual.)
- *Domo arigato* → Thank you. (More formal.)
- *Domo arigato gozaimasu* → Thank you very much. (Most polite; suitable for most occasions).
- *Sumimasen* → Excuse me; I'm sorry; I need to excuse myself; thank you for your trouble.
- *Mo ichido itte kudasai* → Please say that again.
- *Yoroshiku* → Please take care of it; please keep me in mind; it was nice meeting you. (Literally, "Take care of me.")
- *Yoroshiku onegai shimasu* → Please take care of it for me. (For polite requests. Literally, "I beg of you.")
- *Hai* → I see; I hear you; I'm listening; I understand; OK; yes.
- *Iie* → No. (This word is rarely heard, as it is considered too direct. Instead, one generally hears *Chigaimasu* which means "It's different" or *Muzukashii*, meaning "It's difficult.")
- *Chotto* or *Chotto matte (kudasai)* → Wait a minute (please).
- *Ikura desu ka?* → How much is this/that?
- *(Shibuya) (made) wa ikura desu ka?* → How much is (the fare to) (Shibuya)?

- (_____) *wa doko desu ka?* → Where is (_____)?
- *Nani?* (Or, more politely: *Nan desu ka?*) → What?
- *Ja, mata ashita (aimasho)* → See you again tomorrow.

Remaining Healthy and Safe

The phone number for emergencies is 119. Japan is one of the safest countries in the world, with respect to crime. On the other hand, there are the dangers of big-city air quality, crowded streets, and packed trains. More rarely, you might encounter earthquakes, volcanoes, typhoons, tidal waves, fires, floods, and mudslides. Here are a few notes on the most prominent of these phenomena.

Typhoons

Typhoon season runs from July to the end of September. There are as many as twenty in any given season, but there are usually about ten major ones. If a typhoon hits in your location, think hurricane: this is serious business. Forget braving the outdoors with only an umbrella. Better to stay indoors and batten down the hatches. The NHK TV channel will have frequent updates on the storm. All forms of transportation are likely to be shut down, taxis disappear, and major airports are likely to be closed for hours at a time. Just ride it out. The day after it blows through, try to get yourself to the top of any of the city's taller buildings and the view will be spectacular. If you are in Tokyo, it might be the only glimpse you get of Mt. Fuji. Tokyo Tower, Sunshine 60 in Ikebukuro, or any of the skyscrapers in Shinjuku are good vantage points.

Earthquakes

Given that Japan is located at the meeting point of three tectonic plates and has hundreds of identified fault lines, it is possible that you will experience an earthquake while in Japan. Wherever you stay, it's a good idea to make a mental note upon arrival about where the exits are and if there is an emergency evacuation procedure. You will more than likely only feel a slight swaying sensation, much like a train or large truck passing through in close proximity. In fact, you might not have even noticed it as an earthquake until you see it on the news later on.

If it is a truly noticeable earthquake, the rule of thumb is to get under a table or open a door and stand in the doorframe, as it gives you better exit possibilities, or stand in the closet, where the walls are closed in and might have a better chance of withstanding the stress of movement. Most fatalities from earthquakes actually come from the fires that break out afterward and can't be put out due to disruptions in water lines. That is why it's important to know how to get out of the room calmly and quickly.

Buildings in Japan are subject to strict earthquake safety regulations. They are built to sway slightly.

Volcanoes

Japan has several active volcanoes. They are far removed from urban areas, so the chances of being near an erupting volcano are pretty slim. Check with your hotel or place of business if you have any concerns.

Medical Concerns

The American Pharmacy, near Tokyo Station in the basement of the Marunouchi Building, 2-4-1 Maruno-uchi, Chiyoda-ku (tel. 03-5220-7716), carries many typical American medicines—for a price, of course. Japanese doctors will be happy to issue prescriptions, but they will need to know the chemical name of your medication.

If you do find yourself ill, the hotel is the best place to start—they might even have on-site medical personnel. Don't expect any fluency in English at pharmacies (except at the American Pharmacy) or clinics and hospitals in Japan. You may want to bring someone along who can interpret.

Should You Get into Real Trouble: When in Doubt, Apologize Profusely

In the unlikely event you should find yourself in serious trouble, legal or otherwise, you may need to call your embassy. In the back of this book you'll find useful numbers to call for emergencies and various sorts of information, such as select embassies, business organizations, Tokyo English Lifeline (an information hotline for English speakers), and more.

In dealing with any kind of trouble, the best first step, regardless of who is at fault, is to apologize profusely for "not understanding the customs in Japan." Unlike in the U.S., where taking on responsibility can end up costing you the roof over your head in legal fees, in Japan lawsuits are rare. People find court proceedings embarrassing and tend to settle out of court whenever possible, because a court battle reflects badly on all parties involved, no matter who is to blame. If you are in a situation where the police are involved, it is best to show contrition by apologizing. Apologies in Japan function less as admissions of guilt than as acknowledgments that harmony has been broken. In fact, if the police don't sense responsibility being taken on your part (whether you are actually in the wrong or have simply been involved in a situation of harmony being broken), you could get into even worse trouble. If you insist on your innocence, you may be giving the impression that you lack maturity, consideration, or even common decency. Even if the other person is clearly 100 percent at fault, don't be too determined to prove your own innocence. Work patiently with the people involved to realize a reasonable solution.

Use this as your wallet-sized emergency phrase list—copy, cut out, and take it along.

Emergency Phrases

- *Tasukete kudasai.*
    - → Please help me! (For severe cases only.)

- *Tetsudatte kudasai.*
    - → I need a little help.

- *(ABC) hoteru wa doko desu ka?*
    - → Where is the (ABC) hotel?

- *Kibun ga warui.*
    - → I'm ill.

- *Byoin e ikitai desu.*
    - → I need a doctor. (Literally, "I want to go to the hospital.")

- *Saifu/pasupouto o naku shimashita.*
    - → I lost my wallet/passport.

- *Denwa wa doko desu ka?*
    - → Where is the telephone?

- *Otearai wa doko desu ka?*
    - → Where is the restroom?

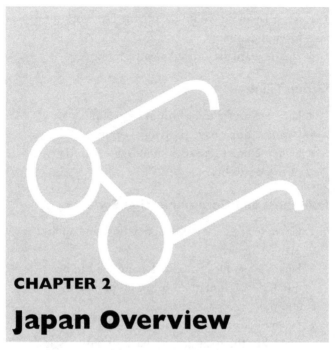

CHAPTER 2

Japan Overview

Here, information on Japanese geography, society, economy, and thousands of years of history are condensed into a few concise pages. We start with a few of the stereotypes and myths many hold about Japan and the Japanese.

Impressions and Misconceptions about Japan

Have you heard any of these? Is there any truth to them? Do you also hold these impressions or stereotypes?

Anti-foreign

- The Japanese market is basically closed to foreign goods.

- Most Japanese would be ashamed to work for a foreign company.
- Japanese are prejudiced against foreigners.

Group Think

- Japanese prefer to do things in groups.
- Japanese don't have individual opinions.
- Japanese don't like to take individual initiative or responsibility.

Politeness and Communication Style

- Japanese are very polite. They bow and apologize frequently.
- Japanese people are very shy and tend to be quiet. They hesitate to speak up in meetings, and they never ask questions.
- Japanese loosen up and let their hair down "after five," but the next day, it's back to business as usual, as if last night had never happened.

Society and Work

- Japan is a stoic, samurai-like society.
- Japanese work long, hard hours.
- Japanese do not make quick decisions. They always rely on consensus.

Society in General

- Japan is a male-dominated society. Women are seen as inferior.
- Japan is changing: it has become very Westernized in the last ten years. They are more like us now.

As you go through this chapter and move into the chapters on business and communication strategies, be alert for clues as to the origin of stereotypes such as the ones above. Also consider how your natural cultural tendencies might have contributed to forming these impressions. To balance the scales, we hope you will also consider what foreigners must look like to many Japanese.

Country Profile

It is important to keep Japan in perspective, to ensure that you do not under- or overestimate the country. Here are some useful details about the country:

Geography

Japan is 376,520 sq. km (145,374 sq. mi.), slightly smaller than the state of California. Japan consists of four major islands: Hokkaido, Honshu, Shikoku, and Kyushu. In all, there are some three thousand populated islands in the country. Only about 11 percent of Japan's land mass is arable. Much of the rest consists of rugged mountainous terrain.

Geology

Located at the conjunction of three major tectonic plates, Japan is subject to frequent earthquakes, close to 1,500 a year. Very few can actually be felt. Quakes of the magnitude of the Kobe earthquake of 1995 happen once every fifty years or so. The country also has numerous volcanoes, mostly inactive, and is vulnerable to *tsunami*, or tidal waves.

Climate

Japan has a relatively mild climate, with hot, sticky summers and cool winters. The main islands of Honshu and Kyushu get only occasional snow at the lower elevations, but the mountain regions get hit with heavy, often wet snowfalls throughout the winter. Hokkaido, in the far north, experiences fairly severe winters with plenty of ice and snow. In contrast, Okinawa and other islands in the far south have a semitropical to tropical climate.

Population

Japan's population is approximately 127.7 million (2006 estimate). Of this population, about 20.8 percent is over 65 years old, one of the highest percentages of senior citizens of any country in the world. From 2001 to 2006, the number of persons aged over 100 doubled to 29,000. The life expectancy, 81.15 years, is one of the highest in the world. The population is 99 percent "pure" Japanese, and about half of the foreigners in Japan are Korean. They might even be fifth-generation Japanese-Korean, but are still considered foreign.

Population Change

As of 2007, Japan's population may actually be shrinking. Japan's birth and death rates have remained low for the last few decades. Japan has also experienced a slight net population loss through emigration and a declining birth rate. In recent years, in order to offset the stagnating growth rate and to have a workers' pool to take on less desirable jobs, immigration programs have been set up to bring in Japanese-Brazilians, Japanese-Peruvians, and others of Japanese ancestry living outside Japan.

Religion

While most Japanese do not consider themselves to be religious, over 80 percent of the people observe either Shinto or Buddhist practices, and usually both, although typically in a very informal fashion. The rest of the population that practices other religions includes a very small Christian minority.

Regional Economies

Over half the population resides in the narrow corridor from Tokyo to Osaka, and most of its industry is centered in these two areas. But areas around less frequently visited cities, such as Nagoya, Hiroshima, and Sendai, are also heavily industrialized. For example, the economy of the northern Honshu region alone is equal to the entire economy of Switzerland.

Administrative Structure

Japan operates through a strong, centralized government, with forty-seven prefectures providing local civic administration.

A Concise History of Japan

Evidence of Japan's long history is juxtaposed with the ultra modern. It's not at all uncommon to see ancient temples sprinkled in among brand-new skyscrapers. Japan, with its five-thousand-plus years of history, reveres its past to a degree that few outsiders can truly appreciate. Going to Japan and not knowing anything of its historical roots is a recipe for looking unschooled and even arrogant. Conversely, knowing something about the history is sure to elicit respect.

Japan goes back so many thousands of years that archeologists still unearth ancient implements from places like Asuka near Nara. There's a bit of controversy involved in these discoveries, in that the further back Japan goes in its history, the more Korean and Chinese influences become evident. Given the less-than-cozy relationship between Japan and these countries, such discoveries are not always met with great fanfare.

Following is our condensed version of more than five thousand years of Japan's history.

Japan's Story of Creation

One of the best clues to determine what is important in a nation's culture can be found in its creation myths. Amaterasu, the Shinto Sun Goddess and spiritual mother of Japan, is said to be a direct descendant of Izanagi and Izanami—the pair of sibling divinities who created the landface of Japan. It's ironic that a nation dominated by men should have a creation story that gives top billing to a goddess. Amaterasu's great grandson, Jimmu Tenno, is said to have ascended the throne to become the first emperor of Japan on February 11, 660 BC. Even today, Japanese use a yearly calendar that follows the year of the current emperor's rule. Noteworthy here is that, according to Japan's creation myth, the imperial household has been an unbroken line descending from Amaterasu. This myth held sway well into the early development of Japan as a nation and was reemphasized during the nationalistic years of World War II to justify Japan's wartime actions as a matter of divine right.

In fact, there were many tribes occupying the islands of Japan for thousands of years, some of them from the north, probably Russia, and others from the south, such as Okinawa and other Pacific islands. Most came from China via the Korean Peninsula, notably the Yamato tribe, from which most modern Japanese are descended.

Timeline of Major Periods and Events

Pre-modern History

3000–300 BC Jomon Period—hunter-gatherer-fisher stage.

300 BC–AD 300 Yayoi Period—start of rice cultivation, advanced pottery techniques, cast iron, and bronze. Animistic religions, later to become known as Shinto, flourish.

AD 4th–7th Centuries Yamato Japan—first sense of a unified nation, under Prince Shotoku.

552–645 Asuka Period—a time of borrowing from perhaps the greatest empire in the world at the time, China. As a result, Japan consolidated its existing power structure and added a level of aesthetic and scholarly sophistication. The principal philosophical borrowings were Buddhism, which had originated in India, and Confucianism, which had originated in China, both in the sixth century BC.

Key figure in this period: Prince Shotoku, who instituted Buddhism throughout Japan and wrote Japan's first constitution in 604. This document reflects Shotoku's substantial borrowing from the highly centralized Chinese governmental structure, with its Confucian virtues of sincerity, form, and ritual, and his view of Buddhism as a peaceful, unifying religious force. The first article is taken directly from the Analects of Confucius, emphasizing harmony and avoidance of conflict.

Prince Shotoku is referred to as a leader who heralded a new spiritual and political era of peace and prosperity in Japan.

Prince Shotoku sent several delegations to China to get the latest word of developments on the continent. He had a protocol of addressing his letters "from the emperor of the rising sun to the emperor of the setting sun," assuming himself to be on equal footing with the ruler of the greatest empire on earth. This did not amuse the Chinese emperor, who was used to absolute subservience from foreign rulers.

710–94 Nara Period—cultural borrowing from China continues. Nara is the capital, modeled on Chinese city planning, with straight roads and well-appointed castles and temples.

794–1185 Heian Period—a kind of Renaissance period for Japanese arts such as literature (*The Tale of Genji*), calligraphy, and painting. Tea was introduced from China. The capital is moved to Kyoto.

After this relatively peaceful era came the Warring Kingdoms, a time of great civil disorganization. The shogun (the top feudal lord or general) leveraged military might to take on political prominence, overseeing the loyal warrior class, or samurai, who carried out his commands and fought his enemies. While the shogun established his seat of power in Kamakura, Kyoto remained the official capital.

1192–1573 Kamakura and Muromachi periods.

1500s Against a backdrop of political disunity and cultural growth, the reunification of Japan proceeded in the latter half of the sixteenth century. Three names stand out: Nobunaga Oda, Hideyoshi Toyotomi, and Ieyasu Tokugawa. They are so famous in Japan that they are often referred to by their first names. Nobunaga never actually became shogun himself but dominated his time, ruthlessly massacring thousands. Hideyoshi completed the reunification of Japan and had such delusions of grandeur that he even made a failed effort to subjugate Ming Dynasty China. Ieyasu employed at least one Englishman, Will Adams, whose story was made famous by James Clavell's novel *Shogun* (and the subsequent television miniseries of the same title).

Another major event took place in the middle of the sixteenth century: the arrival in Japan of Portuguese missionaries and Dutch and Portuguese traders. At first, the missionaries were received warmly and entire areas, especially in southern Japan, converted to Christianity. Gradually, however, the shogun and other feudal leaders became suspicious that the trading ships would be followed by military might. So they outlawed Christianity and all foreigners. This policy of isolation was so strict that, by the 1630s, no foreigners were allowed in Japan, and Japanese who were overseas were not allowed to return.

1603–1868 Edo Period—the policy of isolation held for nearly 250 years, with only a limited number of Dutch and Chinese trading ships allowed to dock at the small island of Dejima in the bay of Nagasaki.

Modern History

1853 Commodore Perry arrives in Japan—"The Black

Ships"

Perry bypassed Nagasaki and sailed directly into Tokyo Bay with his fleet of four ships, including the first two steamships ever seen in Japan. The arrival of these powerful American ships was a startling wake-up call for the reigning shogun. For the first time in some three hundred years, Japan was forced to open up its shores and to interact with the rest of the world. Japan still refers to the "Black Ships" as an expression meaning pressure from the outside.

The Meiji Restoration—a period of total transformation from feudalism to a modern industrial nation.

Key figure in this period: Yukichi Fukuzawa, who learned Dutch and English, traveled abroad, and eventually founded one of Japan's leading institutions of higher learning, Keio University.

1904–5 Russo-Japanese War, which Japan won, thereby alerting the rest of the world to its emergence as a power to be reckoned with.

1927 Notion of the "Greater East Asia Co-prosperity Sphere," which became a part of Japan's rationalization for annexing Taiwan and Korea as virtual colonies and eventually invading other countries, including China. From Japan's point of view, its actions were in part to keep up with the European colonization of Asian countries such as Indonesia, Vietnam, and Hong Kong, and to avoid being annexed themselves.

1931 Japan invades the region of Manchuria in China and sets up a puppet state.

1937 Full-scale invasion of China. By 1938, Japan is effectively under military rule and the divinity of the emperor is reemphasized. *Zaibatsu*, huge industrial conglomerates, are formed to marshal all efforts toward implementing the Greater East Asia Co-prosperity Sphere.

1941 U.S. imposes a total trade embargo on Japan, including oil, which threatens to stifle its military machine. Japan responds in December by launching an attack on the U.S. naval fleet at Pearl Harbor and invading U.S., British, and Dutch possessions in the Pacific.

1942 Japan loses the decisive battle at Midway, turning the war around.

1945 Huge U.S. bombing campaign wipes out most major cities and industrial centers in Japan, including Tokyo. Japan perseveres in an almost suicidal effort not to endure the shame of failure. In Okinawa alone, two hundred thousand perish. The war ends when the U.S. drops atomic bombs on Hiroshima and Nagasaki; the emperor announces surrender and renounces his divine status. His radio-broadcast surrender speech is so eloquent and formal that some Japanese who were hearing his voice for the first time are actually unsure if it meant Japan had lost. Japan is placed under U.S. military occupation led by General Douglas MacArthur.

The *zaibatsu* conglomerates are dismantled, but eventually replaced with new industrial groupings known as *keiretsu* (see page 75).

1952 Treaty of San Francisco, which determines Japan's

postwar constitution and builds a foundation for Japan's political relationship with the rest of the world.

1964 The Tokyo Olympics—by now the world is seeing the economic miracle of full recovery from the devastation of WWII and an enviable industrial boom.

1971 With the Nixon Accord, Japan goes off the gold standard—yen goes from a fixed 360 to the dollar to a floating rate.

1973 Oil crisis hits—economic growth is cut drastically, energy conservation becomes an economic necessity, and government redirects industrial efforts to focus on high-tech industries.

1976 Lockheed scandal rocks Japanese politics, implicating then Prime Minister Kakuei Tanaka and shaking the Liberal Democratic Party stronghold.

1979 Second oil crisis. Power-saving products boom.

Mid 1980s "Bubble Economy" takes shape.

1989 Death of Emperor Hirohito, the longest reigning sovereign (sixty-four years) in Japanese history. Emperor Akihito ascends to the throne. Bribery scandals hit Japanese politics hard.

1991 Bubble Economy goes bust and Japan enters a new era of restructuring and deregulation.

1995 Kobe earthquake kills more than five thousand people. An errant religious cult, Aum Shinrikyo, stages a terrorist attack on major subway stations in Tokyo, killing about a dozen and injuring thousands of rush-hour commuters. Yen rises to its highest rate ever, hitting 77 to the dollar in early 1995.

1998 Winter Olympics are held in Nagano, Japan.

1999 Japan places huge capital investments in the new Internet economy in sometimes nonexistent net companies, creating a "Net Bubble."

2000 Prime Minister Keizo Obuchi dies while in office and is replaced by Yoshio Mori. Late in the year, the "Net Bubble" bursts, sending Japanese tech stocks plummeting. Japan experiences a record number of bankruptcies. The wireless revolution inundates Japan, with iMode customers topping the 10 million mark.

2001 Junichiro Koizumi becomes prime minister in April. In contrast to his predecessor, Koizumi is wildly popular amid hope that he will effectively tackle Japan's economic malaise. The long-awaited first child (a girl) is born to Crown Prince Naruhito and the popular Princess Masako, but the question of imperial succession remains, as law requires a male heir. Mad cow disease scare causes consumption of beef and meat products to plummet.

2002 Prime Minister Koizumi's inability to make headway on promised reforms severely damages his popularity. Makiko Tanaka, Japan's first female foreign minister, is summarily fired. Japan hosts the World Cup (soccer) jointly with Korea for the first time.

2003 Japan participates in the war in Iraq, raising questions about Japan's military role and the Japanese Constitution which prohibits Japan from using military force. With such high population density, Japan worries about an epidemic from SARS, mad cow disease, and bird flu. China's economic power increases. Rise of Japanese baseball stars in U.S. Major Leagues.

2004 Japan heats up (literally): record heat waves cause concern about global warming. Tension begins to rise between Japan and neighboring countries still feeling that Japan has not properly addressed issues related to WWII.

2005 North Korean isolation, poverty, and military ambitions destabilize regional security; their kidnapping of Japanese citizens in previous decades is exposed. Economic recovery slowly ramps up, private investment increases. Privatization of the Japan postal service, which is also the largest savings deposit bank in the world, begins. iMode services reaches 50 million customers worldwide.

2006 A baby boy is born to Prince Akishino, second in line to the imperial throne, thus ensuring a potential male heir to the throne. China begins to overtake the U.S. as Japan's biggest trading partner. Japan's interest rate increases for the first time in six years indicating greater economic stabilization. Transition from Prime Minister Koizumi to Shinzo Abe. As the ninetieth prime minister, Abe is the first to be born after WWII.

2007 Car maker Toyota outsells GM for the first time. Number of iMode customers reaches beyond the 80 million mark. First of WWII baby boomers begin to retire amid a scandal of millions of lost pension records. Prime Minister Abe abruptly resigns and is succeeded by Yasuo Fukuda.

Society, Politics, and the Economy

1
2
3
4
5
6
7
8

Society

Consider this: If 80 percent of the population of Japan lives on 20 percent of the land, it would be like cramming the combined populations of Germany, Spain, and Ireland into a space about the size of England. Such density virtually obligates people to be group oriented and space conscious. Harmony and stability—not individualism—become key values. The postwar Japanese economic miracle has been possible due to the hardworking "salaryman," who has traditionally devoted his entire working life to one organization. Group or company affiliation describes who one is as a person. There's a high emphasis on education; diligent study is required to get into the best universities, which are conduits to the most desirable companies. The work ethic is strong and the savings rate is high. Women often make many of the decisions regarding both the education of their children and household finances.

Politics

Even Japanese will roll their eyes here. Politics haven't changed much in the years since WWII, because stability is so important that no one risks change. The Liberal Democratic Party (LDP), which despite its name is conservative, has dominated the political scene since the mid-1950s. Japan can be properly defined as a constitutional monarchy with the emperor as figurehead over a parliamentary government. The legislative body is called the Diet and is bicameral. In addition to ongoing economic doldrums, there have been numerous payoff and kickback scandals in recent years. As a result, the Japanese have become somewhat cynical about politics and have lost faith in their politicians' ability to change the situation. Former Prime Minister Koizumi fought an uphill battle for meaningful reform—his results were less than anticipated. His predecessor, Prime Minister Abe, who appeared to have strong pro-Japan aims, resigned in September 2007 amid accusations of financial scandal. Yasuo Fukuda, son of a former LDP prime minister is confirmed as the new prime minister.

Economy

Even after the burst of the bubble economy, Japan still maintains the world's second-largest economy. A spate of books by Western observers was written in the bubble years of the 1980s to analyze Japan's superior manufacturing techniques. Some Japanese concepts made their way into our business vocabulary and were imitated on assembly lines the world over. Ironically, not all these concepts were originally Japanese. The Deming Award for Total Quality, for example, honors an American, W. Edwards Deming, whose ideas were initially all but ignored in the U.S. but immediately accepted in Japan.

Here are some of the more familiar Japanese concepts that have in some cases become adopted worldwide:

- *Kanban*: An assembly-line system in which production can be halted at any time by the line worker if a defect is detected.
- *Kaizen*: Small, continuous, incremental improvements that lead to a zero-defect rate.
- Just in Time: A top-to-bottom manufacturing and delivery system which strives to keep excess inventory at near zero.
- TQC: Originally a Deming concept, Total Quality Circles in which line workers get together to find new ways to improve production.

- *Keiretsu:* Tightly knit industrial conglomerates, which are in many ways a carryover from the prewar *zaibatsu* groupings. *Keiretsu* have served as a source of vertical integration, industrial strength, and financial security for its constituent members. Each has generally included an automobile manufacturer and a large institutional bank. Mitsui, Mitsubishi, and Sumitomo are some of them. It has never been easy for outside companies, whether foreign or Japanese, to penetrate these closed corporate networks. Recently, however, the *keiretsu* system is weakening to some extent. The share of business that *keiretsu* companies do with each other has been diminishing, and the partnerships that they've been forming with outside companies have been increasing.

Japan's Role in Asia

While no one would doubt that Japan stands out as an economic and cultural powerhouse in Asia, most Japanese people would refer to the rest of Asia as some other "foreign" place, very much in the same way the U.K. refers to Continental Europe. Japan's aggressive actions in WWII have left some permanent scars in Asia. Political relations with many Asian countries remain strained, making it challenging for Japan to take on a visible regional leadership role. At the same time, trade and business between the countries continue to increase at a record pace. Japan remains the unquestioned benchmark of quality and technology. For all the challenges of doing business in Japan, it is in some sense the model for and gateway to all of Asia.

Understanding business practices in Japan should be your first step in any strategy for business success in Asia.

CHAPTER 3

Business in Japan

As we fully enter the twenty-first century, globalization has become more than just a buzzword for many companies large and small. But we still haven't figured out how to make globalization work in practical terms. Undoubtedly, Japan represents one of the most important but most difficult "players" because of its culture and its own unique preferences for how to get things done. Therefore, no matter what precautions are taken, there is usually some frustration in doing business in Japan. Non-Japanese often experience this in a lack of productivity or in wasted resources. Whatever the actual cause of the frustration, we often blame what we see as Japanese foot-dragging, hyper-caution, and/or perceived "incompetence." Japanese dislike the haphazard approach of their overseas counterparts, or even more typically, blame their own lack of English skills. This chapter zeroes in on the causes of frustration by addressing the critical issues of business and culture.

Here are some business-related questions we often hear from our Japan-bound clients:

1. Can I conduct business in Japan pretty much like I do in Portland, London, or Mumbai?

2. How do I handle the business-card exchange—do I have to speak in Japanese?

3. Do I really have to bow? Don't most Japanese shake hands?

4. Do I have to go out drinking every night? What if I don't drink?

5. Is it possible for a foreign woman to close a deal in Japan?

6. Why do decisions seem to take so long in Japan?

7. Why don't they just say "No" if that's what they mean?

8. How do they ever get things done over there?

Read on for answers to these and many other questions you might have on business conduct and doing business in Japan.

Hosting, Gifts, Business Cards, and More: Following Business Protocol

"I'm the kind of person who is a mover and a shaker—I can go to Japan and get things done, turn things around." If this sounds like you talking, you just might want to re-think your strategy. Ignore protocol in Japan at your own peril. Deeply embedded in the Japanese psyche is a sense of the way things ought to be done. Japanese common sense, or *joshiki*, means knowing that there is only one right way to do something.

Mastering Japanese protocol would take years of practice, so don't lose sleep about getting every detail right. If you make an attempt to practice certain protocols, you will win the instant admiration of your new Japanese colleagues and partners. In Japan, the game is to try to put everyone at ease and attend to their comfort, rather than just getting down to business. Of course, doing business as usual with no attention to protocol is always an option. At best, you will make your hosts uncomfortable and will possibly be seen as inflexible and difficult. At worst, you will be unsuccessful in your business dealings.

> Visitors to Japan, especially U.S. Americans, tend to want to make their own choices at restaurants; to have everything already decided can make some feel shackled, as though personal preferences don't matter. This is why the guest-host scenario in Japan can sometimes bring on distress rather than the intended feeling of comfort. Remember that for the Japanese, letting the uninitiated guest experience the discomfort of making tough decisions about unfamiliar food would be considered upsetting and rude. For the guest, the path of least resistance is to go with the flow.

Hosting and Being Hosted

Hosting is almost an art form in Japan. Here are some assumptions regarding hosts and guests:

- The host should make things look as smooth as possible.
- There should be no surprises!
- Taking care of someone should be all inclusive—no time should go unplanned.
- Anticipating needs—always be one step ahead of any eventuality.

- At dinner, guests should be seated in order of rank, with the senior person in the middle on the side farthest from the door.
- At dinner or a nightclub, the host is expected to pay for dinner or drinks out of sight—no discussion of bills or checks should take place in front of the guests.
- When bidding farewell, the host should accompany guests until they have departed and are out of sight.

Guests

- Avoid awkwardness at all cost.
- Communicate in advance to your Japanese hosts details on the gender, ranks, and roles of all in your party; let them know who is in charge, and whether anyone is allergic or unable to eat any food item.
- Graciously accept what is served.
- Show appreciation by thanking your hosts several times for their fine hospitality, if possible in Japanese, and apologizing for any trouble you might be causing them.
- Bring gifts—as a way to balance the inevitable effort that will be shown to the guest.

Zen of Gift Giving

Around the world, Japanese are known for bolstering local economies with their expenditures on gifts. On returning from trips, they bring back gifts to family and, more important, to colleagues and coworkers inconvenienced by their absence.

Gifts will usually not be opened in the giver's presence, so in some situations it could be embarrassing to insist that a gift be opened.

What Sort of Gift Is Appropriate?

Consider the following:

- It's less a present than a courtesy, a concrete way to show appreciation for your host in anticipation of the courtesies that will be shown to you during your stay. It shows forethought, in the same way that you wouldn't show up at a U.S. barbeque without a six-pack or something in hand. Thus, a company memento, such as a unique pen that is nicely crafted is the order of the day. These days, thinking with some creativity is welcomed.
- The gift should be easy to carry and wrap, and not take up too much space.
- Elegantly packaged cookies, chocolates, tea, or other items that can be shared with a group are always welcome.
- Something that represents your local area, for example a (small) photo book of your city or state, locally made goods, or (packaged) foods.
- Certain functional items such as small handmade crafts or ceramics, elegant hand towels, or brand-name money clips.
- On subsequent visits, feel free to personalize your gifts more: NY Mets or Seattle Mariners caps for the work group, for example, or logo T-shirts for your counterparts' kids, a jazz CD for the guy you know to be a big fan, a bottle of scotch, a sleeve of golf balls from a famous course or with your company logo. The usual upscale items sold through duty free might be a practical choice.

- A really good gift: A framed photo of the last event together with a note about how much you enjoyed the visit.

Appearance of the gift is as important as the gift itself. Having it wrapped properly makes a good impression. Think form over content. As a last resort, you might be able to get it wrapped at your hotel in Japan.

Disaster presents: Avoid items that are large, hard to divide, garish, or cheap-looking. Don't give large jugs of maple syrup, items made in Japan or other Asian countries, cutting implements, including knives, letter openers, pocket knives, (which could represent a severing of the relationship), craft items that might take up a lot of space, or elaborate jewelry or loud clothing, such as a Christmas sweater with a big reindeer on it. Also, Japanese will avoid giving things in sets of four, since the sound of the word "four" (*shi*) can also mean death.

Examples of gifts you might receive, usually beautifully packaged and individually wrapped: Cookies and sweets, often representing a particular region or famous hotel, *osembei* (traditional rice crackers), green tea, *omanju* (rice cake with sweet bean paste inside), craft items, pens, chopsticks, fans, *furoshiki* (beautiful scarves used to wrap presents), *sake* sets, souvenirs, packets of postcards, trays, or teacups.

Remember, one thank you is not enough. Offer your thanks more than once in perhaps a couple of different ways. In addition, follow up afterwards with a note or an e-mail that indicates what you received. When meeting that person again later, it would be good Japanese form to start out by thanking them again for the lovely gift, even if it was over a year ago!

Please note that the prolonged economic downturn

in Japan has made gift giving less lavish and expected than before. Check with your inside sources before making your decision on what to bring. In high-tech, design, or Internet-related industries where corporate cultures are relatively informal as compared to older-line Japanese companies, gift giving may have gone the way of the VHS.

Let's Bow on That

You may think you can get away with not bowing, but by refusing to bow, you may be sending an unintended message of defiance, arrogance, or lack of common sense and courtesy—not exactly the way to put your best foot forward! By making the effort to bow, however awkward, you will instead both show respect and elicit it from your Japanese associates. Bowing is so full of variations and attendant meanings for the Japanese that there is no need, however, to mimic all its subtleties. Instead, you can show your politeness and effort to adapt to Japan by just bowing one time slightly, keeping your eyes down and your hands still at your sides. Making strong eye contact while bowing is done only in the martial arts, before squaring off for a fight. In business settings, always acknowledge another's bow by bowing back. No need to worry about bowing as low as the other person.

> **Factoid**
> If you are actually invited to someone's home, one suggestion would be to bring an attractive-looking dessert for everyone: decorated cakes, pastries, a bottle of your favorite wine, or nicely packaged fruit. If you bring flowers, stick with long-stemmed arrangements, but no white or yellow chrysanthemums, which are for funerals, or red roses, which would be considered mildly romantic.

Japanese do shake hands, though some may not be prepared for the Western-style handshake; it's not an automatic business protocol for them. The best approach here is to extend your hand just as you would in most other countries. Japanese are often seen bowing and shaking hands simultaneously—we would encourage you to respectfully reciprocate. Note that handshakes in Japan are generally weak and might also take a week! Some Japanese don't know the cues about adjusting one's handshake to the firmness of the other person or even when to stop. In general there is little physical contact in Japan in most professional and social situations. Eye contact is also not as intense—think "soft eye contact."

Business Card Exchange

Business cards, or *meishi*, and the ritual of exchanging them are de rigueur in Japan.

Preparation

As noted in Chapter 1, be sure to have an adequate supply of cards, many more than you might think necessary; it's bad form to run out. Keep your cards in a dark-colored leather cardholder. If you forget to bring it, you can usually purchase one at an airport shop. Ideally, the cards should be printed in both English and Japanese.

The Exchange

Business-card exchange in Japan occurs at the beginning of any interaction, not at the end (as happens on occasion in many other countries outside of Asia). Treat business cards seriously and respectfully, like a gift—they are far more than just an information reference, they represent the person and are symbolic of their "face." Make sure your cards are in mint condition, and keep the cards you receive well organized.

First-Time Meetings

Keep the cardholder in an inside pocket. Women can carry it in a handbag or purse, having it easily accessible for the moment of meeting. Avoid searching your pockets or digging around in a bag, when you should be bowing, business cards at the ready, and giving a good impression.

Presenting the Card

Remove your card from the holder, hand it with both hands to the person at chest level or lower so they can read it without having to take the card and turn it around. Say your name and company name when extending the card. Even though you may have already stated your name earlier when you came in the door, say it again for confirmation. The receiver will usually receive the card with both hands and will spend a few moments studying the card. It's polite for the receiver to read the name aloud to confirm pronunciation

> **Factoid**
>
> Many new hire manuals in traditional Japanese companies recommend that one look at the other person's neck or tie knot, to avoid sustained eye contact. This can be potentially disconcerting, especially if you are a woman dealing with a Japanese man. You may feel he is looking at you inappropriately. Don't be overly concerned; he might actually be attempting to show respect by *not* meeting you eye to eye.

and to make some comment. For example, on the name they might remark, "Is this a German name?" or, "Am I pronouncing your name correctly?" Regarding the title, "So you are the R and D director?" When Japanese exchange cards with each other, it's not unusual to discuss the meaning of the Chinese characters of Japanese names. People also might ask about the address: "Oh, so you're from San Francisco. It's a beautiful city," etc. This is a great opportunity to establish possible common topics, and is often the starting point for building good business relations.

Receiving the Card

If possible take it with both hands. If the exchange is simultaneous, receive it with the left hand while giving your card with your right hand. Study it for a few moments. At least attempt to pronounce the last name, and remember to add "-*san*" after the name. It's OK to struggle with it and let them help you. Repeat the name until you feel you've said it correctly. When you are seated, it is customary to place the cards you have received on the table as a kind of seating chart. Leave the cards there for the duration of the meeting. Please don't fantasize that you are a blackjack dealer and toss out cards around the table, as can happen in the U.S. In addition, don't scribble on the cards while the persons from whom you have re-

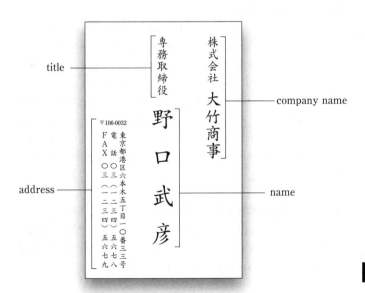

ceived them are present; do not fold them; and don't put them casually in your wallet and stick it in your back pocket. Hardly a show of respect for the "face" of your associate!

Minimum Graces

Don't worry about getting every detail of the ritual perfectly—what's more important is to make the effort to respect this custom. Have plenty of cards, and give them out with respect. Study the cards you receive. Help the recipients pronounce your name, and attempt to pronounce theirs. This approach will go a long way toward developing productive business relationships.

Seating Arrangements: The Door and More

Imagine yourself the head samurai in need of vigilant protection from enemies. Where would you sit to have the best protection? Far from the door, facing the door, in the middle of the table. This may be one of the only cultures where "showing you the door" implies that you are the respected one. Your hosts may very well go through some ritual of seating you across the table and in the middle. The one near the door would be the most junior and expendable. If in doubt about where to sit, whether at a business meeting or at a restaurant, it's best to wait until a Japanese directs you. This goes for seating arrangements in cars as well. It's considered good form to let the VIPs sit in the back seat, and if it's full, the host sits in the front by the driver.

The Office Environment

If you get the opportunity to take a tour of a typical Japanese office, don't miss it. What may hit you immediately when you walk into a large office is the open-floor plan, sometimes devoid of windows. Most Westerners would find it far too public a setting to work in, but the Japanese prefer it to a more closed environment where information might not flow as easily and there is little sense of cooperation or open communication.

Various Japanese industries, particularly in the fashion and high-tech worlds, might utilize alternative office layouts. Ironically, the cubicles, which started out in U.S. companies as a way to reduce walled barriers and open up the office environment, have the opposite effect in Japan of creating more privacy.

This preferred arrangement enables information flow. Japanese employees perform their functions within this often noisy informational network. The excuse "No one told me that," which might be uttered by U.S. workers about not having some specific piece of knowledge, wouldn't elicit sympathy in Japan. The Japanese take pride in their perceived advantage of having free-flowing, nice-to-know information that enables them to stay abreast of important business activities and company news. When so much of company life is audible, visible, and literally taking place so closely around you, it's no wonder that the Japanese have an easier time knowing what others are doing, or not doing, and what the status is on any given project, proposal, or sales transaction. Some U.S. companies are even considering moving to the open-style Japanese-like offices in hopes of creating better teamwork and reducing space costs.

Customer Service and the New Temporary Worker—What Used to be "OLs" (Office Ladies)

Certain job categories in Japan may strike you as odd.

Some ubiquitous examples: "elevator girls," colorfully uniform-clad young women, who gracefully escort customers up in department store elevators; similarly clad young women who greet you with polite words and low bows when you enter a department store; and special attendants at service stations who not only put the gas in your car but also risk life and limb to stop traffic and help you get back out onto the crowded road. The extra "caution" sign holders at construction sites. Some might consider these positions to be somewhat superfluous, but in Japan these service personnel are deemed essential to creating the right atmosphere for service.

Another example of what may seem like a relic in most businesses is the "office lady," or OL, young women hired usually by the larger more traditional companies to perform exclusively administrative tasks. These women, often wearing uniforms adorned by a name badge, scurry around making and serving tea and coffee to guests and company personnel, answering phones, making copies, and sometimes running errands for the boss.

From the Trenches

In a recent incident involving a well-known multinational company in Japan, one new foreign manager found that he couldn't cope with the cacophonous arrangement existing in the Tokyo office. He requested a high-walled cubicle. Naturally, this was met with a great deal of resistance from the Japanese staff. It took weeks for them to understand that he wasn't doing this out of arrogance or a desire to cut everyone off, but because he needed more privacy to concentrate and work effectively. Nonetheless, the damage wrought on his working relationships had already been done.

On the opposite end of the spectrum, "rewarding" your Japanese employees by kicking them upstairs to a private office may be met with great resistance as they will feel cut off from the essential information flow and marginalized from their point person role.

When working with newer, high-tech companies or foreign capital companies in Japan you might not find any OLs among the female staff. Not only are budgets in Japan bare bones these days, but the women who join these types of companies are generally more career-minded and seeking functional rather than form-related tasks. Some of these women specifically look to join companies with automatic tea dispensers so as to side step the whole tea-serving issue. The OL function has been replaced in large part by contract workers and *haken*—temporary workers hired through an agency. This has become the norm.

Basic Body Language

You will be regarded in accordance with your image—attire and behavior count. In Japan, your body language will likely be seen as "loud" compared to the more subtle Japanese style. So try to keep your body quiet: slow down, keep your voice tone low, limit facial expressions, and greatly reduce your hand gestures. In fact, Japanese could become so distracted by vigorous hand gestures that they may not pay attention to what you are saying. When pointing, instead of using just your index finger, use your whole hand with open palm. Also, avoid shrugging, which strikes Japanese as odd. They will take meaning from body language, even if you intended none.

Regarding facial expressions, the pleasant gentle smile is key. Many Japanese will maintain this kind of smile, even when embarrassed, angry, or conveying bad news. Maintaining this type of facial expression will help make any situation more comfortable.

On posture, it's best to keep the body a little more contained and dignified than usual. You might notice that Japanese men have a very crisp, rigid form to their bowing and seating postures. Following their lead will give your Japanese counterparts more reason to be comfortable with you and to respect you.

The most respectful posture, invariably taken by vendors visiting customers, is to sit on only about the front two-thirds of the seat. Avoid touching your back to the back of the chair and crossing your legs, unless you are seated at a table. When making presentations, use only your chair as a seat, not the table or desk. If you put your feet up on the table or desk, you will become an instant—and odd—legend.

TIP: Learn to read between the lines—become aware of not just your own body language, but really tune in to the nonverbal communication of your Japanese colleagues. From time to time you will need to sense the general atmosphere of the room—disagreement may be in the air, but not actually specifically verbalized. See more on deciphering "Yes" and "No" in the next chapter on communication.

Thanking and Apologizing

As we've mentioned a few times before, always thank your hosts. Then thank them again. As part of your expression of thanks, include an apology for causing them trouble at a busy time.

Upon meeting a second time or more, Japanese typically thank each other for whatever they may have done since the last time as a kind of conversation opener "Thank you for (what you did) last time . . . " This practice holds even if the last time was two years ago. This conveys that neither the gesture nor the relationship has been forgotten.

Meetings

At a first meeting, the key objective is to begin the relationship by getting to know each other, so hard business issues are rarely discussed. For the Japanese, this approach is not extraneous to the business, nor is it fluff: it is the business. When major problems crop up, formal meetings may not be the place where the problem solving gets done but where the problem is acknowledged and the team that will do the work is announced. The nuts and bolts of the acknowledged problem will then be tackled in subsequent, less formal meetings.

The preference in Japan is for no surprises or major disagreements to come up in formal meetings. Actual and potential disagreements would have been hashed out on a more one-to-one basis, before the "real" meeting takes place. The Japanese refer to this approach as *nemawashi* (a concept which will be explained in more detail in the "Key Japanese Concepts for Business Conduct" section; see page 130), which is the groundwork needed to align everyone involved in the project before a meeting. This practice cannot be skipped in doing business with Japanese. As a result, the formal meeting, especially if it involves both insiders (the Japanese company you might be meeting with) and outsiders (you, the foreign entity), will appear to be just a rubber stamp on decisions already made behind the scenes. At such meetings, a senior person might do most of the talking, even if he or she is not the person doing the actual work of the project. As much as possible, address the senior person rather than directing your conversation toward the interpreter, or toward the person you might have been working with up to this point. In Japan, the formal meeting may be the place to confirm what has already been agreed to via the *nemawashi* process. In meetings you can share and impart important information, and expect the audience to take copious notes. Sometimes they are concentrating so hard their eyes are closed. It's reasonable not to expect much Q and A. That might happen afterward or during a break.

Make no mistake, in Japan the official meetings serve the important purpose of finalizing agreements and plans and demonstrating commitment, so to think you can skip them because no decisions are made or "nothing gets done" would be a fallacy.

Tip: Carefully plan meetings in advance by sending a detailed agenda to your Japanese partners. Ask for their input. Check their level of alignment with the various items and try to work through any potential problems. You might want to have one or more pre-meetings via teleconference, before arriving in Japan for a face-to-face meeting. Also, clarify among your team members the roles each will have at the meeting. Be ready to defer certain difficult or perhaps delicate agenda items to after-hours socializing or other less formal opportunities in between meetings. The more groundwork you are willing to do, the less time you'll need to spend on impasses over seemingly small items during your formal meetings. It'll be worth the time investment—and far more cost effective than having to spend extra days in Japan!

The Business of Entertaining

Business entertaining is the means of building relationships in Japan. The amount corporate America spends on lawyers roughly equals the amount that corporate Japan spends on entertaining. The question we might grapple with: "Litigate or inebriate?"

What about mixing business and pleasure? One U.S.

client told us he might have ten items on his agenda in Japan, but only brings up five of them in the "official" meeting. The other five he saves for the after-hours period. While out enjoying an evening of karaoke and camaraderie with his counterparts, he manages to get the other five items addressed.

While the economic downturn and subsequent restructuring has caused some belt-tightening, Japanese businessmen are known for their readiness to plunk down huge sums on dinners, drinks, karaoke, sumo wrestling matches, extravagant gifts, baseball games, and golf excursions. The spirit of serving through entertaining is still pervasive in Japan. Just when you think you're finished with a lovely dinner, you might be invited out to a *nijikai* (second party) for drinks, often at a hostess bar. On occasion, there could actually be a "third party," although many of our Japanese associates have told us that it's not the mandatory marathon that it was just a few decades ago. Many non-Japanese are either unprepared or weary of this tradition of very long evenings. It may be tempting to opt out from the beginning—but don't deny yourself these important relationship-building opportunities. While business dinners in the U.S. typically end in mid-evening, in Japan you could find yourself returning to your hotel well after midnight. Here's what you can do to avoid overdoing it:

- Pace yourself when it comes to alcohol. At dinners, Japanese may begin with beer, then order sake, unless they're having Western food and wine. Since Japanese etiquette requires that you pour for others, not for yourself, your hosts will frequently refill your glass—even when it is not empty. So it's best to "nurse" your drink over time, taking only small sips, and enjoy the lively conversation and people in your group.

- When someone offers to refill your drink, lift your glass and tip it slightly toward the proffered bottle as an acknowledgment of the courtesy you are receiving. Then return the favor by filling the glass of the person who just filled yours. Be vigilant to make sure that the glasses of the people sitting around you are filled.

- At a bar (whether piano or hostess bar or kara-oke), many Japanese will opt to drink scotch and water. You can always request your hostess to fix yours with a lot of water.

- If you don't or can't drink, for whatever reason, you won't be alone. Many Japanese these days are paying closer attention to health consider-ations and cutting back on alcohol. Generally you have two alternatives. The first is to allow your glass to be filled and simply not drink from it. Most Japanese will quickly notice this and ask if you would prefer a soft drink. The second is to say that your doctor has told you not to drink alcohol. But the practice of pouring for others— you pouring beer for them and they pouring a soft drink for you—still holds.

At some Japanese dinners, the diners themselves might be engaged in the food preparation. The waitress will serve the ingredients, but it's up to those at the ta-ble to prepare the entré (*shabu-shabu*, for example). The point here is to join in and enjoy a relaxing group process. While doing this, many Japanese will want to discuss the food and the health attributes they provide. For example, did you know that *konnyaku* (a type of vegetable root) is good for your intestines, or that seaweed is good for your hair, or that liver is good for your eyes? Conversations like these abound in Japan; they are not only of real interest to Japanese but they are also safe topics for a mixed crowd. You can learn about the wide array of food consumed by Japanese, and at the same time you might want to offer insights about food from your own country or region. Participating in the atmosphere of the evening in this way goes a long way toward making your Japanese counterparts comfortable with you and to cultivating productive business relationships.

TIP FOR BUSINESSWOMEN: We are often asked to what extent women going to Japan on business are expected to partake in the after-hours socializing as well, and what to expect. By all means, we encourage businesswomen to join in on the relationship-building activities outside of work, certainly for the first round. Keep your sense of humor when dealing with your possibly tipsy colleagues. Show that you are part of the team, and that you have a personal stake in the success of both the business and the relationship with your Japanese colleagues as well.

Determining Who Pays

The person extending the invitation in Japan is generally expected to pay. Exceptions include a colleague who is just asking you to dine with him/her for lunch, or friends who, instead of splitting the check, opt to take turns paying. If you are dining with government officials, you will usually be expected to pay. In the case of a work group, the bill may be split evenly. The concept of separate checks (*"betsu betsu"*) is relatively uncommon, except for more daily situations such as lunch with your office colleagues. Playing the role of the host in Japan includes paying for everything in many cases, even the taxi fare your guest will incur returning to their lodging. Many companies arrange for taxi vouchers, which can be used to pay the fare.

If you have been entertained to such a royal degree that you feel obligated to reciprocate before you depart, invite your Japanese colleagues/counterparts to lunch or dinner and make sure they understand that it will be your treat. This gesture, which can also take the place of a physical gift, will be greatly appreciated. You can ask one of your Japanese colleagues to recommend a restaurant, if you don't know one. Following standard Japanese practice, take care of the check during the last course, out of sight of those whom you have invited. Excuse yourself to go to the restroom, and subtly pay the bill to avoid any arguments over the check.

Tatami

Tatami are thick straw mats with a covering of tightly woven rushes that are the traditional flooring in Japanese homes and Japanese-style restaurants and inns. The dimensions of the mats are constant, and the number of mats determines the size of a Japanese room (the most common sizes are four-and-a-half, six, or eight mats). One never walks on *tatami* with slippers or shoes. Socks or stockings are OK, so it's advisable to have good socks in Japan, without any holes.

Tatami matting in a restaurant usually means you will be sitting on the floor on cushions called *zabuton*. Be prepared for this possibility by wearing appropriate clothing. If you have back trouble or extra long legs, be sure to let your hosts know so arrangements can be made.

Many restaurants have a lowered portion under the table for easier upright seating.

Chopsticks

Chopsticks are the main eating implements in Japan. For the uninitiated, however, it can be a real challenge to use them skillfully, especially when trying to pick up unrecognizable and slippery food items. Practice will help, of course, but if you find yourself failing to transport food to its proper destination—your mouth—please do not resort to spearing your food. For the Japanese, this would definitely be a barbaric act. Don't be surprised if your Japanese host, noticing your struggle to use chopsticks, has the waiter bring you a knife and fork. While this could seem somewhat disappointing, since you may feel that your success with chopsticks is just around the corner, your host is not trying to show you up. Rather, Japanese common sense is to alleviate a guest's discomfort. To do otherwise would be considered rude. Apologize for your inability to use chopsticks and have a sense of humor about the situation. On the other hand, any dexterity with chopsticks will probably elicit a number of compliments by your Japanese dining companions.

What to Expect: Wet Washcloths, Slurping, and No Napkins!

The approach to eating in Japan may strike you as different as the food itself. In many restaurants, for example, you will be offered an *oshibori*, or wet washcloth, hot or cold, depending on the season. (The hot towel you receive on long international flights is a practice borrowed from Japan.) It is a way to clean your hands and refresh your face. Once it is taken away by the waitress, you will realize that there may not be any napkin to place in your lap. This custom is reserved mostly for some Western-style or family restaurants. Most Japanese carry a hand-kerchief and notably women unfold theirs in their lap as a napkin replacement. Feel free to ask for another *oshibori*, if necessary. You will see some napkins in a holder on the tables in some restaurants. These napkins are quite tiny and best used not to put on your lap but for wiping around your mouth during and after your meal.

Eating with gusto is also a regular part of the dining experience in Japan. Japanese often make slurping noises when they eat, especially soups and noodles in hot broth (such as *soba*, *udon*, or *ramen*). This noise can unsettle those from cultures where eating quietly is the rule. In Japan, however, slurping is an auditory signal that the food is good and also serves to cool the noodles and broth as they make contact with your tongue. In fact, by not slurping you may be signaling that the food is not all that tasty. Here is a case where mirroring the Japanese style will gain you substantial cultural points.

Karaoke

Karaoke (pronounced "kah-rah-o-keh," not "carry-oh-key"), literally "empty orchestra," is a popular group activity, in which individuals take turns singing to taped accompaniment. The portion of the lead singer is deleted, leaving you the opportunity to assume that role. For some of us, the prospect of singing solo in public seems rather daunting, on the order of death and taxes. But remember that in karaoke individual virtuosity or ineptitude is irrelevant. What is relevant is the group activity. In other words, participation in and with the group is key.

For non-Japanese, you will no doubt find all of your favorites, from the oldies but goodies to whomever might be popular at the moment. The advent of DVDs and wireless technology have added many practically limitless choices to the song menu, depending on whether you're in the mood for Elvis or Green Day. Choosing from familiar songs means you'll be able to sing along with the lyrics as they pop up on the video monitor facing you. By the way, the videos that go along with the song may have little to do with the song lyrics, and might even classify as adult content.

If you still feel overwhelmed by the prospect of standing in front of people you barely know, holding a mike and singing, you can ask one of your Japanese colleagues to sing one of the pop songs in English with you as a kind of duet. This could be flattering for the one asked and you might feel support sensing that your voice is masked a bit by your partner's. It can be great fun and those watching get as much of a kick out of the situation as the singers.

For the Japanese, karaoke is a way to bond with colleagues through an entertaining and stress-relieving group activity. If you sit there and refuse to sing, you single yourself out as an unwilling member of the group in Japan. As you will soon realize, Japanese applaud any singer heartily, no matter the quality of the singing, both after the first stanza and at the end. Oh, and don't hog the microphone, either.

Beyond Karaoke

You might have the privilege of being invited for an outing or even a weekend trip, possibly to play golf and/or enjoy Japanese hot springs. Like the late-night carousing, these extended trips are not as common or as frequent as they once were, but when they do happen they can be rather involved affairs. (For details on both of these activities, see Chapter 7, "Beyond Survival: Exploring Japan.")

The golf question is easy enough. A round of golf is usually planned weeks or months in advance, can last all day, beginning with breakfast, then the front nine, then a sumptuous lunch, then the back nine, then a relaxing Japanese bath. In addition to adhering to this rigorous schedule, remember that it's not considered good form to beat the most senior person. Golf in Japan is a rather expensive proposition, but it provides an excellent relationship-building opportunity.

As for hot springs, Japanese may well assume that the world would be a better place if everyone could have a hot spring or *onsen* experience at least once in a lifetime. Hot-spring resorts are often in picturesque sites, with baths both inside and outside. The experience can be exhilarating and you might be surprised at how open and relaxed your counterparts—and you too—become when soothed with the warm, healing waters from deep within the earth. Be sure to check out our section on the hot spring bathing experience and protocol in Chapter 7.

Strategies for Success in Japan

In this section, we will explore some important strategies for business success in Japan, including prominently the critical issues of human interactions across cultures.

Educational Underpinnings

The Japanese educational system underpins the business world. The system is centralized through the Ministry of

Education, with a uniform curriculum for all schools. A school kid could move from one side of Japan to the other and pretty much fit in without missing a beat. Compare that to the U.S., where there are fifty different educational systems, one for each state, with vastly different emphases. Japanese kids go to school about 210 days per year, in contrast to about 180 per year in the U.S. The Japanese curriculum places heavy emphasis on mathematics and the sciences, although reforms in 2002 simplified the curriculum substantially. However, former Prime Minister Abe proposed reforms to make education more rigorous again. The curriculum is carefully designed to prepare kids for standardized tests. Starting as early as kindergarten, these tests occur at each subsequent level and will determine where students rank within their school, and, in succession, what elementary, junior high, or high school students qualify for, and what university they might attend. With the strict ranking of universities, the name of your school will, for the most part, determine what companies will recruit you and how far you might be able to climb in society.

As a result, the Japanese system is geared to absorbing raw knowledge, and there is a lot of it. Japanese graduates simply amass more factual information than their Western-educated counterparts. However, when it comes to applying that knowledge to analyze problems and make quick decisions, it seems that Western educational systems have the upper hand. Quick analysis, the case study approach, and critical decision making hasn't been part of the traditional Japanese educational curriculum, and yet these are the business skills that are critical to success in the constantly changing, high-tech, global business world.

Possible Gaps in Business Practices

Concepts we might assume to be common sense in the supposedly international business world, such as individual accountability, taking individual initiative, and being proactive, run counter to Japanese common sense—i.e., the notions of harmony, stability, and consensus building. Japanese, therefore, may respond quite differently when faced with completely new endeavors or with problems to solve. They are most comfortable when they have a set model or very specific directions about the "proper" way to execute a task. Foreign managers in Japan often complain about having to spell everything out for their Japanese subordinates when approaching a new project or initiative. And Japanese employees often feel frustrated when their foreign manager hasn't provided them with either a model, a format, or specific instructions. Without such guidance, they may be concerned that they are being set up for failure.

Showing and Gaining Respect with Your Japanese Counterparts

Everyone cites mutual respect as essential to business success. Yet, how respect is shown and gained across cultures is not universal. Consider these questions: Do you show someone respect by delegating all decisions to them or by taking initiative to solve your own problems? Should you be assertive or deferential? Should you be self-confident or diffident? Is it best to exude gentle optimism or cautious realism? Should you highlight your own accomplishments or demonstrate humility at every turn? The strategy you have adopted consciously or unconsciously for showing and gaining respect might or might not lead to success in Japan.

What to do? Following are some quotes to frame the tandem issues of credibility and respect in greater depth.

Concerns of Westerners Going to Japan

- "I'm really worried about offending people."
- "I don't want to look bad or ignorant."
- "How do I cultivate credibility?"
- "How will I be perceived?"
- "How will I know if the Japanese accept me?"
- "How will I get results?"

Concerns of Japanese Going to English-Speaking Countries

- "I'm really worried I won't get all the information because of my bad English."
- "I will make a fool of myself, I'll embarrass myself and my company in front of a group."
- "Without good communication, how can we build a relationship?"
- "Without a good relationship, how can we do business?"

These quotes reveal the difference in assumptions in the West and Japan about how to show and gain credibility and, hence, respect, which, of course, are required to successfully conduct business. Using the U.S. as a contrasting example, the chart on the next page illustrates some of the finer points of showing and gaining credibility in both countries. Use this as a steppingstone to the following chart, on respect.

As you can see from the above examples, "common sense" notions about building credibility are anything but common. You'll note that many of the contrasts come in the way a leader would be viewed: good self-starter or good team player? Think about your own culture or corporate culture. How does one build credibility there? Is it more like the U.S. or the Japan model?

Respect and Credibility

Respect and credibility are two sides of the same coin. Credibility is the foundation for respect; showing respect for others is integral to successful business dealings. As

Credibility in the U.S.	Credibility in Japan
Show confidence; toot your own horn.	Show modesty, be subtle; let someone else toot your horn, and you toot theirs.
Maintain integrity; strive to be consistent with your values in all situations.	Be willing to adjust to the situation, show flexibility.
Set challenging goals, take risks, take initiative.	Be cautious, consider all potential ramifications before taking action.
Show your competency (individual capability).	Show your sincerity (concern for others).
Be visible; take a leadership role.	Blend with the group; lead from behind the scenes.
Convey enthusiasm and/or passion.	Convey personal commitment.
Be "honest": tell it like it is, whatever the consequences.	Be "honest": avoid embarrassing others, maintain harmony at all cost.
Bring in the external "experts," lawyers, and consultants to show seriousness of purpose.	Bring in a large internal entourage (never lawyers) to show seriousness of purpose.
Gain respect by building credibility.	Gain respect by allowing others to confirm and support your credibility.

with credibility, there are many ways of showing respect, many of which are culturally bound. Essential here is awareness of how your behavior impacts the other person. Remember that our behaviors are largely determined by our respective cultural upbringings.

Showing Respect in the U.S.	Showing Respect in Japan
Be yourself, don't be a phony; talk about accomplishments.	Use an appropriately polite tone; downplay your accomplishments.
Treat others as equals; establish a friendly atmosphere; use first names.	Show respect for status, age, seniority; demonstrate your knowledge of the other person's background.
Be positive at a first meeting (e.g., "Jill says such great things about you.")	Show your knowledge of the other person's organization and its history.
Talk about goals, future possibilities, and paybacks.	Talk about the background of the partnership.
Elicit opinions, ask questions, challenge opinions.	Listen intently and say as little as possible.
Get down to business; don't waste time.	Show willingness to build a relationship.
Show interest in the other's current work initiatives.	Show understanding of the other's situation and adjust accordingly.
Challenge their ideas.	Harmonize with what they say.
Give praise; acknowledge others' individual achievements.	Acknowledge group achievements.
Give frequent feedback.	Be neutral, save face, find the right timing and place to give feedback.
Create your own persona: what you say and do is who you are.	Your persona is created in and through the group: you are who they think you are.

Tips on How to Show and Gain Respect in Japan

- Listen to others very carefully.
- Develop your ability to read between the lines—take everyone's needs into account whether they are expressed or not.
- Show your sincerity in making everyone feel comfortable with the business at hand.
- Demonstrate your seriousness of purpose in a tactful way.
- As a leader, provide direction; don't expect Japanese employees to jump in and take initiative when it comes to solving problems and making decisions.
- Provide direction, but don't do all the talking.
- If you are the leader, don't feel you need to chime in on every point—more talking does not equal greater authority in Japan.
- Be realistic, not superficially optimistic.
- Don't say, "Yes, yes, yes, we'll do that," when you know it might not happen.
- Refrain from boasting of your own individual accomplishments and abilities. A leader is sup-

Factoid

When the late great film director Akira Kurosawa (*Seven Samurai*, *Kagemusha*, etc.) gave his acceptance speech for the Lifetime Achievement Award at the Academy Awards, he started out by saying, "I still have a lot to learn about filmmaking . . . " The audience assumed it was a joke and laughed accordingly. There was a tense moment between the interpreter and Kurosawa, who was wondering if the interpreter had gotten the message right. But Kurosawa was merely following the wisdom of the Japanese proverb: "The mature rice plant bows its head." So his intention was far from humor—he was being sincerely modest about his achievements.

posed to have extensive knowledge and experience but modestly proclaim that he or she is still learning.

TIP FOR BUSINESSWOMEN: To build credibility and respect, perhaps the most important first step is to make sure your role and your bandwidth is crystal clear. There are very few women who make it to the ranks of upper management in Japan. As both a foreigner and a woman, you are likely to be a bit of a curiosity for some of your Japanese counterparts, who might not have had much experience dealing with professional women beyond their administrative staff. It won't help if they are surprised when a woman shows up, especially if you look younger than your peers in Japan. You will improve your chances of a positive reception if your role is clear to them, they know something about your work style, personality, and even your appearance, in advance. To further bolster your authority in their eyes, arrange to have your American team members defer to you when strategic questions arise and decisions are called for. As in any country in Asia, watch out for appearing to be overly authoritative and demanding.

Finally, don't offer to help with the tea, coffee, or copying since such activities are likely to be performed by support staff in Japan. Allow your Japanese counterparts to accord you status. Even if you feel any disrespect, it's best to keep your sense of humor and keep your emotions in check. By all means, avoid going on the defensive as that tactic rarely works in Japan. With the right balance of patience, determination, and composure, businesswomen can certainly close the deal in Japan.

Concept of Face

You've probably heard something about the Asian concept of "face," which is the way someone is perceived publicly (i.e., one's reputation). In most Asian countries, your "face" and your credibility are synonymous. With a proper introduction, you may not need to do much more to "sell yourself." One's "face" has direct bearing on one's credibility. Japanese, living in a society where appearances really count, are quite sensitive about face. If you cause someone to lose face, which generally means public embarrassment, you yourself can lose credibility.

Here are some scenarios in which face will probably be lost:

- Reprimanding an employee in front of his or her coworkers.
- Scolding a vendor for delivery problems and/or poor quality in front of the team.
- Correcting someone's mistakes in front of his or her colleagues.
- Challenging someone in a meeting with colleagues present.
- Upstaging someone at an event.
- Implying that the company you are meeting with "needs help" or is not very well known.

Building Face

Here are some ways to build face and simultaneously bolster credibility with your Japanese counterparts:

- In a one-on-one situation, praise your Japanese counterpart's accomplishments.
- Help others build their network through respectful introductions.
- Praise the team, even when an individual did most of the work. Singling someone out could create embarrassment for that person.

- Praise the Japanese company with which you are doing business at appropriate opportunities.
- Apologize for the inconvenience when things have gone awry, and assume a share of the responsibility.
- Understand that apologizing is considered polite, professional behavior.

In certain litigious countries, such as the U.S., fear of ending up in the courts often restricts the use of apologies. This is not so in Japan, where apologizing is a minimum course of action to maintain harmony—especially in cases where face may have been lost. In any case, going to court in Japan is widely considered an embarrassment as bad or worse than whatever damage or hurt has been inflicted.

Presenting Information

Mindful of differences in logic formation and information organization, non–Japanese may need to modify how they present information to their Japanese counterparts in order to ensure mutual understanding.

Japanese often say they appreciate how Westerners in business are so logical, almost as if to imply that they themselves are somehow not so logical. Westerners doing business with Japanese often cite their frustration at the perceived illogic of certain Japanese courses of action (or inaction). But isn't the way different people organize and express their thoughts, like most other patterns of behavior, culturally bound? Indeed, most Japanese words for and related to "logic" can sound cold and calculating and are not necessarily positive.

How Information Is Organized

In the West we learn a particular style of writing: introduction, thesis statement, body with supporting evidence, conclusion. In a U.S.-style MBA course, one uses roughly that same style for case-study analysis: introduction, problem statement, supporting evidence and analysis, conclusion and recommendation. In business writing, we learn that if our conclusion/recommendation/solution isn't in the first line of the memo or e-mail, the rest of the memo might go unread. The typical complaint we hear from our U.S.-based clients about working with Japanese is, "Why the need for so much extraneous detail?"

For many Japanese, what is considered "rational" or "logical" is based on being consistent with one's current context. Logic is based on adjusting to current circumstances, rather than adhering to some unchanging, abstract set of principles.

Japanese are taught in their early schooling to follow a model that traditionally has been based on *ki-sho-ten-*

From the Trenches

One U.S. manager was getting pressure from his boss to motivate his Japanese counterpart to follow the company's standardized reporting protocol. During several trips to Japan, the U.S. manager repeatedly asked the Japanese manager to change his reporting approach, giving very clear guidelines. The Japanese manager dutifully proclaimed his agreement, but as soon as the U.S. manager left Japan, he went straight back to his "old ways." When the U.S. manager learned about the concept of "face," he decided to change his approach. On his next Japan trip, the U.S. manager explained, "Because you're doing things in this way, my (U.S.) boss is losing face." This prompted sudden and meaningful change on the part of the Japanese manager—who at last understood the gravity of the situation for the visiting U.S. manager. While this approach might not work in all situations, it demonstrates an effective cultural solution to a tricky business problem.

ketsu, or introduction, body, example, conclusion, which has its origins in Chinese philosophy. From the outside this may look somewhat familiar. But consider how it plays out. *Ki* sets the tone and should include considerable background. *Sho* involves development of the topic within the stated context, with examples. *Ten* gives "by the way" background details and/or alternative examples. *Ketsu* is the conclusion, which, given the background and examples already presented, can be vaguely stated, perhaps as a question, or even omitted. The Japanese assumption is that the audience can figure it out based on the context.

Here's an example of how *ki-sho-ten-ketsu* thinking might be expressed in a business situation in Japan. "A" is a manager wanting to set up a meeting to discuss the next product. "B" is the engineer responsible for fixing the glitch in the previous generation of the product. The dialogue might sound like this:

A: Could you participate in a meeting next Thursday evening on the new product launch?

B: Well, as you know, for the last several weeks, I've been working very late everyday since the glitch was detected. Our main customer, Yoyota, could have a lines-down situation, if this problem is not corrected before launch. So if we are thinking about next Thursday, we need to consider whether or not having a meeting is possible. By the way, we must consider that Yoyota has a factory visit scheduled for late next week. So, maybe . . .

From the explanation of the situation, "A" should "logically" conclude that Thursday is not a good day for a meeting, and offer to reschedule.

The indirect approach to communication can lead to problems when interacting with cultures with a more direct style. The clear preference in many Western countries is for the "straight" answer, directly given, with supporting examples; background details are offered only as needed.

Without complete context, however, Japanese may find it difficult to understand the meaning of a communication. As a result, they are accustomed to providing extensive background details which may not appear to be in any order. So, while the conclusion may not be immediately clear, all of the possible variables that could factor into it are thoroughly addressed.

In the heavily U.S.-influenced international business style, executives typically have scant patience for hearing all the background details. They are constantly aware of their tight schedules and wonder loudly, "Where are you going with this?" or "What's your point?" The dominant concern is far more the task at hand and desired results than the context or the process. For credibility in a business setting, one might try to "shoot holes" in someone else's theory and indicate bluntly what should be done instead. That would hardly be conducive to effectiveness when working with the more detail- and context-oriented Japanese, who will demand that the topic be analyzed from the whole range of data points.

TIP: When presenting information in Japan, try to switch to a more contextual mode. Take time to set the stage with some background details and information about the history of your relationship before launching into your bottom-line conclusion.

TIP: Consider creating a presentation template. Sometimes it works really well to formulate a format or template for more routine presentations, such as status updates. This gives your Japanese partners a guideline or boundary as to what information you will be expecting, and also helps them to follow your logic.

TIP: Be a patient listener. Wait until your Japanese colleagues finish what they are saying before clarifying points or asking for conclusions. If you are in an extended relationship, help them understand the way you like to organize information. You might consider using a roadmap analogy to describe what you mean: "When I get information from you, it's like we're reading a roadmap together," "It helps me to know the destination before I can easily follow along with you." On the other hand, Japanese need to know as much as they can about the terrain they'll be traversing before setting out on a trip with you.

TIP: Use charts, diagrams, photos, cartoon representations, product samples, scale models, and other visual aids to support and explain your spoken message. Be ready with back-up slides or handouts, as your Japanese audience might request the background details on your bulleted slides. Translate written materials into Japanese and make sure that all handouts are of uniform quality and appearance.

Information Sharing

Japanese appear to exchange information somewhat more freely and easily with their work associates than happens in many other cultures. This is partly owing to the particular Japanese need for context and to their strong collectivist leanings. The Japanese approach to information sharing stands in stark contrast to the U.S. approach, which can be characterized as hoarding information to protect one's turf and sharing it only on a need-to-know basis.

Your Japanese colleagues will expect information that you may consider to be proprietary or extraneous. This is not an affront, an attempt to rob the store, or an effort to simply annoy you; it is, rather, an expectation based on a very real need to have a complete picture and to be ready to answer all questions that the customer or other related parties might have for them. A recovery plan from a product defect or failure will typically include a very detailed root-cause analysis, no matter what the costs in time or resources, and sometimes even for products that are no longer in production. This attention to detail is what has made Japan the leader in manufacturing and production.

Giving and Receiving Feedback

With global teams expanding and increasing in number, the expectation for giving and receiving immediate feedback across borders has also increased. Understanding how feedback is handled in Japan is a must if we expect to work effectively with our Japanese team members.

These are some typical, maybe even stereotypical complaints made by non-Japanese about getting feedback from their Japanese counterparts:

- "The Japanese are reluctant to provide immediate feedback."
- "They don't say 'No.' So it's unclear when the news is bad."
- "Japanese push back from 'new' ideas."
- "I don't know what the Japanese are really thinking about."
- "When they give feedback, it's only negative."
- "They only give feedback after the fact—like after a meeting."

- "Their feedback comes in the form of 'implementation,' with no advance notice."
- "I can't figure out what they are looking for. For example, what response to a customer complaint will really satisfy them?"
- "Their feedback is usually too vague."
- "I can't read them!"

Japanese, on the other hand, grumble about the following on feedback from their Western counterparts:

- "Foreigners don't take context or situation into account. Their feedback is too specific."
- "Westerners' feedback is too confrontational."
- "Their feedback is pointed at one individual only, not the team."
- "Their feedback often results in a loss of face."
- "Westerners' feedback doesn't include the notions of *tatemae* and *honne*." (Public stance and private feelings—see the section in this chapter titled "Key Japanese Concepts for Business Conduct," p. 130.)
- "They need to give more background information."
- "The feedback comes back so fast and furiously it's like bullets."
- "Why are they so pushy?"

Japanese might often assume that the problem should be obvious from the context, thereby making specific comments unnecessary. There's a preference for using either intermediaries or some indirect form of alluding to the problem to avoid direct confrontation.

Tips for Giving Feedback

- Use intermediaries.

- Provide background details.
- Consider ramifications of any "quick fix."
- Don't expect immediate feedback—take a long-term view.
- Think through what you really want to say.

Tips for Getting Feedback

- Think contextually—listen for hints and subtle references to problems. Read between the lines.
- After giving a presentation, instead of asking, "What do you think?" allow people to start the discussion in Japanese.
- Check in with your key Japanese contact and others.
- Arrange for follow-up face-to-face meetings or phone calls with your Japanese counterparts.
- Don't push for specifics.
- Soften requests for opinions.
- Exercise patience.

Negotiating

It is in negotiating with Japanese that many foreigners feel overwhelmed by the Japanese way of doing things. Differences in negotiation style have so stymied some Western companies that they have even packed up and returned home without inking any deal whatsoever. Ultimately, success in negotiating with Japanese will depend on how you undertake the process. In that regard, we are rarely sufficiently prepared.

As Japan is a non-litigious society, the mere presence of an attorney might be perceived as an aggressive move. Japanese may be reluctant to use attorneys, especially at the beginning of a process. It may not help to have an attorney on your negotiating team at the beginning.

Consider the following suggestions:

- Send more than one person. In Japan, whatever the size of the company or potential contract, you will likely be facing a team of Japanese from all levels and all divisions of their company. Show your seriousness and sincerity not by behaving as the Lone Ranger but by sending at least two persons and perhaps more. If necessary, for example, you might send an engineer and a marketing director with a high-level decision maker. Having several members on your team allows you to take turns speaking and time to gather your thoughts and observe the discussion as it unfolds. Those who accompany you to a negotiation in Japan should have good interpersonal skills and be good listeners. These skills are perhaps more important than knowledge of a particular business area.

- Appear as a cohesive team. Japanese are quite adept at creating what appears to be an "unbreakable front" at the negotiating table with their sense of proper deference and respect toward each other. Notice that no one will interrupt another person. Follow this cue.

- Assign roles to the members of your team. Everyone on your team should have specific roles: leader and spokesperson, manufacturing director, technical expert, and so on. Plan carefully what each one will contribute to the negotiation.

- Listen carefully to what your counterparts are saying. Think about what they are saying and how they are saying it. Don't interrupt.

- Modify your English. Address questions and concerns with utmost sincerity, using English sentences that are clear, short, and easily understood. It's quite possible that your counterparts may not speak English well or that you will need to use an interpreter. Therefore, slow the pace, pausing often. If you notice that what you have said hasn't been understood, offer to explain that particular thought again. And instead of, "Do you understand?" ask, "Is my explanation clear?" or "Would it be helpful if I explained this point again?" or "Shall I give you an example?" This is a courtesy that puts the onus of clarity on the speaker, not the listener.

- Do your research and planning before stepping on the plane. Have you taken a look at the annual report of the company you will be meeting? Have you done some research on the Web about their business? Who are the people you are meeting? Have you asked for their bios? Who will be at the negotiation table? Has an agenda been agreed upon? What are the maximum and minimum figures or terms you will offer or accept? Think about sending an agenda, which can be modified by your Japanese counterparts, before any face-to-face meeting occurs. Proper preparation before entering Japan will enable you to appear well informed and ready to do business. In short, you need thorough knowledge of the specific Japanese company and, more broadly, of the industry in question. For example, what obstacles and pressures is your counterpart facing in Japan and what are they trying to accomplish in Japan and/or Asia?

- Summarize major points after ample time has been spent addressing them. Get group buy-in along the way.
- Avoid brainstorming with Japanese at the negotiating table. The place to think openly with the Japanese team about new alternatives or dilemmas is away from the negotiating table and should be done in a casual, informal manner— perhaps during a break, or even over a meal or drinks. (See the section on the Japanese concept of *ba*, p. 138–39.)
- Bring all kinds of data with you. Make sure that everything is in writing, easy to read, and that there are enough sets for everyone at the meeting. Written documents should be translated into Japanese whenever possible. (Also, remember that your Japanese counterparts will assume that what is in writing is true.)
- Spend time setting the stage for your proposal. Especially in the U.S., we tend to focus logically only on the immediate issue, the benefits, and bottom line. You will get a better hearing in Japan, however, if you spend time reviewing the background of your company and your relationship, even if brief, with your prospective customer or counterpart and how the proposal on the table was developed. In addition, express your gratitude at being able to meet with those sitting across from you.
- Be prepared to apologize whenever necessary. If a misunderstanding occurs, or if new facts are

being introduced which are contrary to what has been sent earlier to your Japanese counterparts, an apology is in order. It constitutes a face-saving demonstration of your sincere interest in the harmony or well-being of the group. Unlike in the West, where we often see apologies as a sign of weakness, the Japanese regard them as a means to ward off potential conflict; apologies demonstrate willingness to continue the relationship and to accept responsibility for any perceived snafu.

- Try polite persistence. Westerners often find Japanese somewhat vague. To get beyond this perception, be as specific and concrete as possible in your questions. It's acceptable to ask the same question more than once to elicit a clear answer.

- Prepare to be asked the same question more than once. The Japanese do not necessarily consider the first answer the final word. It is considered polite to ask the same question again if new information has been introduced into the discussion, if they did not understand the first answer given, or if the first answer was not what they were expecting.

- Rephrase your questions to verify understanding. If, for example, what you have heard appears to be a negative response, you can make certain of the meaning by asking: "It seems that it might be difficult for you?" Then pause and wait for a response. This is a good way to make sure everything is clear and that you and your Japanese counterparts are on the same page.

You know you are making progress in the negotiation when your Japanese counterparts:

- Ask increasingly focused questions.
- Bring in specialists and virtually everyone who would be involved.
- Ask for more details and documents.
- Give more details about needs, desires, expectations, hopes.
- Want to talk about next steps; for example, visiting your company overseas.
- Create more opportunities to socialize and continue relationship building.
- Start to discuss specific commitments (dates, quantities, money).

You are probably *not* making progress when they:

- Ask no questions.
- Make such comments as, "It will be difficult," or "We're thinking about it."
- Suck air through their teeth.
- Feign understanding of what you're saying, while you're pretty sure they aren't following you.
- Give no hint of next steps.
- Do not bring in specialists to assess the product nor introduce you to top management.
- Give no response after the meetings, even after your requests for follow up.

Cautions in Negotiating

1. Don't confuse politeness with agreement. Japanese may remain quite cordial and want to preserve harmony even if they have no intention of working with you.

2. Avoid offering early concessions as a way to get things moving. This approach would strike the Japanese as a sign of weakness or desperation. However, at the end of the negotiation (at a point when Westerners may think the negotiation is essentially over), the Japanese might ask for concessions. This so-called "closing squeeze" is further reason why it would be unwise to make concessions early on.

3. Avoid backing your Japanese counterparts against a wall. To preserve face and harmony, the Japanese need an escape hatch. In fact, the hard sell almost never works in Japan. More than likely it will backfire, and you may never get a second chance. Even if your hard sell does produce a deal, and you go back to headquarters with your "victory," we know of many cases where things start to go wrong after that point. You may find your quick deal falling through.

4. Be prepared for negotiations to continue after the formal negotiations are done. We've heard of cases where "No" is just a starting point.

If you can stick to the basic pointers offered here, you vastly enhance your chances for success. Many West-

From the Trenches

One American manager recalls how he and his colleagues were treated to an extravagant tour of southern Japan by representatives of a potential Japanese partner, complete with lavish meals and accommodations at some of the most expensive Japanese-style inns. By the end of this first-rate tour, the American, who was convinced that the deal was done, was shocked when his Japanese hosts informed him that they had chosen instead to do business with another company. For the Americans, the Japanese decision seemed so inconsistent with the polite treatment that they had been receiving. For the Japanese, this would be consistent with their need to get to know a potential business partner before making a long-term commitment.

ern business executives go to Japan with the idea that they can just "wing it" through the negotiation, armed with their elaborate video-enhanced PowerPoint presentations, in-depth product knowledge, and clever legal counsel. That won't cut it in Japan. Know your audience and your market. Recognize that the negotiation process in Japan will take longer than you think. That's just the way it is. Exercise patience.

Conflict Resolution

Even after the most successful negotiation, conflicts can arise along the way. Here again, the typical Japanese approach might seem very different from what you have practiced or witnessed at home.

In Japan, conflict is avoided if at all possible, rather than met head on. Should you find yourself in, or headed for, conflict, try to think long term and avoid the immediate temptation to hash out differences openly. Here are some tactics you can use to successfully manage or avoid conflict with Japanese:

- Create a comfortable environment with small talk at the beginning of a meeting.
- Keep your reactions, however negative, in check. Maintain a pleasant expression.
- Apologize profusely and as soon as possible; acknowledge the efforts of the other side.
- Be aware of Japanese concerns, such as face-saving, human relations, and the need for harmony.
- Do some groundwork, or *nemawashi*. Gather as much information as you can on what happened and let the other side know about your effort to get at the root cause. Be ready with a recovery

plan. Get information on how the problem has affected, or might affect, the Japan side.

From the Trenches

A Japanese high-tech company and an American supplier found themselves in a serious conflict. The U.S. supplier slipped up and sent a product that was off calibration by an embarrassing margin. This led to a snowball effect of defective products for the Japanese firm, along with a huge drop in their stock price. The U.S. side would have been happy to settle this in court, but the Japan side needed something more. Here is what they were looking for:

1. A sincere apology from the company's top officer in a face-to-face meeting with the Japanese customer.
2. A detailed explanation to specify and analyze the root cause, including all related technical details.
3. A recovery plan with proposed compensation for damages incurred.

By the way, here's what didn't work:

1. Demonstrating confusion: "We're not sure exactly how this happened."
2. Defiance: "I don't see the need to apologize, let's get on with business."
3. Blaming someone else: "We apologize, but it's not our fault—it was our vendor."

- Talk the issue through calmly.
- In particularly difficult cases, consider using a third-party intermediary who is trusted by both sides.
- If you do bring in lawyers they can add clarity to the situation by bringing up key liabilities and potential pitfalls.
- Consider solutions jointly; don't be pushy about having it your way.
- Show effort by offering to take constructive action.
- Be patient always. Assume a patient demeanor, even if you're sweating under your collar.

Conflict in Japan tends to get resolved in indirect ways. Using an analogy: The Japanese manager might say something like, "How is your health?" when what he really wants to get at is, "Why have you been turning in shoddy work lately?" Another common method Japanese employ to avoid conflict is to ignore a commitment, even if you feel they had earlier agreed to it. This is yet another good reason to reconfirm agreements and action steps at the end of a meeting, and to always follow up with written communication afterwards.

Tip: As we've highlighted in previous examples, try using a third party. If things get heated, a traditional tactic in Japan is to prevail upon a third party (though it is unlikely that it will be an attorney) who is mutually familiar and respected to help resolve the situation.

Tip: Try being subjective rather than objective. The art of persuasion in Western countries involves using personal opinion backed by valid, objective evidence. With Japanese you might get further if you don't work so hard to convince them. They prefer using subjective suggestion, such as, "Wouldn't this be good?" or "This one seems to be the best." This more gentle, subjective approach can change the atmosphere and bring you toward agreement.

Decision Making

Decision making in Japan can seem slow and cumbersome by Western standards. The decision-making process generally follows a bottom-to-top path. Of course, the original impetus or directive to pursue the issue comes from the top, but virtually all the action to develop the idea and move it along—from feasibility research to consideration of contingencies to plans for implementation is undertaken at lower levels and gradually pushed up through the organization. By the time the issue reaches the upper echelons, it has gone through intense scrutiny by many persons and has had all the kinks worked out, so the top managers can often just rubber-stamp it. This means that all key players must buy in before an idea is officially approved—a long and arduous process by Western standards. Yet, this system has an incredibly rapid implementation timeframe. You won't want to miss the final "official" meeting.

Ringi: You may find yourself at some point in the midst of the Japanese *ringi* system. This is the process of circulating a proposal, drafted at lower levels, to the various key managers and executives (hence, the movement from bottom to top) with special boxes or circles for each person's personal chop, or seal, to indicate approval. The process can prompt discussion and amendments, but usually it's more of a rubber-stamp process that reflects—and ensures—consensus among all concerned. Be patient. *Ringi* is not a step backwards but rather reflects the forward momentum of your proposal.

Building and Maintaining Relationships

It is generally known that the relationships you build and maintain with your Japanese partners will be critical to your success in Japan. This requires considerable time, but relationships constitute the glue that holds together all other aspects of doing business in Japan; long-term personal relationships often lead to long-term, mutually beneficial business activity.

The relationship-building dynamic congenial to Japanese can be loosely rendered as "meet me, get to know me, trust me, marry me . . . and then we'll do business." That illustrates their need to establish and build rapport prior to transacting any kind of business. It's quite different from the U.S., where business can actually be conducted by people who hardly know each other.

Comparing U.S. and Japanese Decision-Making Steps

In Japan, the plan for implementation may come from the bottom up. On its way up, the decision or initiative will go through several rounds of altering and tweaking until consensus is reached among those involved with or affected by the implementation. While this process can seem unwieldy and time consuming, it can work efficiently, particularly in manufacturing. The implementation stage typically goes more smoothly as everyone is already on board. Many global managers have come to understand that the time to implementation in many cases is shortened by the Japanese approach.

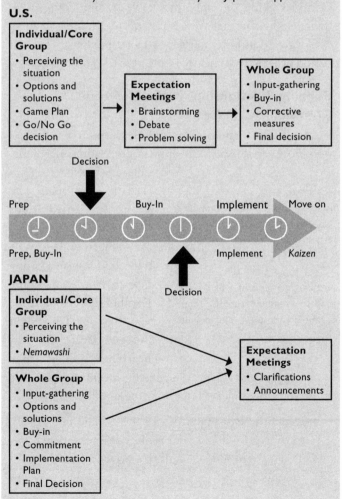

U.S.

Individual/Core Group
- Perceiving the situation
- Options and solutions
- Game Plan
- Go/No Go decision

Expectation Meetings
- Brainstorming
- Debate
- Problem solving

Whole Group
- Input-gathering
- Buy-in
- Corrective measures
- Final decision

Decision

Prep   Buy-In   Implement   Move on

Prep, Buy-In   Implement   *Kaizen*

JAPAN

Decision

Individual/Core Group
- Perceiving the situation
- *Nemawashi*

Whole Group
- Input-gathering
- Options and solutions
- Buy-in
- Commitment
- Implementation Plan
- Final Decision

Expectation Meetings
- Clarifications
- Announcements

1
2
3
4
5
6
7
8

127

Tip: Understand that in Japan, as elsewhere in East Asia, introductions are extremely important and that it may take time to meet a potential partner or customer. The *keiretsu* system of corporate alliances underscores the need for you to cultivate your own set of contacts. For example, meeting and forming relationships with local government officials could lead to strategic corporate introductions. Consider going through a reputable trading company as their relationship network is far and wide. This, in turn, could give you potential access to corporate circles that would otherwise be nearly impossible to approach.

Building Relationships in the Electronic Communication Age

In the age of virtual teams and electronic communication, how can one possibly build good relationships without ever expecting to actually go to Japan? The studies of virtual teams have shown that they are subject to the same trust-building needs of a face-to-face team—quite possibly more so because you have to trust sight unseen. Don't be disheartened. Go to Japan if the opportunity arises, but in the meantime, here are some additional ideas about building good relations.

Manners Matter

In a discussion with a 2007 new hire, we found that his new entry "class" did not even touch a computer or start any "real work" for the whole first week on the job, but spent their time listening to speeches, engaging in small group discussions, meeting senior members of the organization, and building relationships.

- Establish "best practices" for the e-mails between yourself and your remote team members.
- Take care to send e-mails that are clear and easy to follow.

- Include a simple greeting at the beginning and end of your e-mails.
- Send e-mails that include sharing additional information about the industry, the business, your country, or whatever you believe might be of interest to your Japan partners.
- Stay in touch with current events in Japan, and mention stories that you think could affect your colleagues, such as the weather, sports, earthquakes. Show an interest in Japan.
- Pick up the phone and call once in a while instead of just relying on e-mail—this helps them get a sense of who you are.
- Consider a photo wall of all team members—pictures really help.
- When possible, choose video conference over teleconference.

Building Contacts—Where to Begin

If you don't have established connections via your company or organization or mutual associates, start with Japan-related organizations in your home country, such as the Japan External Trade Organization (JETRO), the Japanese embassy or a consular office, your state Japan trade offices, Japanese prefectural trade offices overseas, industry associations with overseas branches (e.g., American Management Association), American Chamber of Commerce in Japan (not just for U.S. Americans), and others in the expatriate community in Japan.

Tips for Maintaining Contacts

- Show an awareness of the time and effort it takes to develop relationships.

- Be aware that the person responsible for making the contact or introducing you is placing his/her own credibility on the line.
- Be mindful of the other person's status, position, and feelings.
- Use face-to-face contact as much as possible.
- Share information widely and frequently.
- Create a comfortable atmosphere through small talk before getting to the business or main point.
- Exchange gifts, as appropriate.
- Work and socialize together.
- Take responsibility and apologize when things don't go well.
- Seek the help of intermediaries when necessary.
- Offer personal assistance to your associates, even with non-business matters, whenever possible— the favor will be noticed and likely reciprocated.

Remember that one of the most important rewards of doing global business is the range and quality of the relationships you create.

Key Japanese Concepts for Business Conduct

In this section we will introduce several key concepts that fall into the category of Japanese common sense. They shape everyday business life in Japan. With a grasp of these concepts and a few insights on related behaviors, you will be able to demonstrate your understanding of basic Japanese business culture, build better relationships, and ultimately enhance your chances of success.

A word of caution: Referring openly to these concepts with your Japanese counterparts would strike them as odd, almost as if you were trying (amateurishly) to psychoanalyze them. While the terms in fact describe what is occurring beneath the surface, the Japanese rarely use them during the normal course of business.

人間関係 *Ningenkankei*: **Human Relationships**

This aspect of Japanese business culture is widely known. It's not extraneous to business transactions but integral to them. The critical commitment here is not to getting the "deal" done but to building long-term business relationships. While common sense in the U.S. has it that "time is money," the Japanese say that "relationships are money." In fact, it is nearly impossible to conduct business in Japan without establishing proper relationships. Your customers are likely to belong to a particular *keiretsu*, or business grouping, with roots extending to the pre-WWII *zaibatsu* (interlocking, cross-shareholding conglomerates, broken up during the Occupation). In the unwritten rules of such relationships, the umbrella conglomerate takes care of its affiliates in hard times and the affiliates treat the larger *keiretsu* companies as senior figures—i.e., with great deference.

TIP: Pay attention to the kind of atmosphere you create when interacting with Japanese counterparts. It should be conducive to building relationships and moving things in the desired direction. What might you do or say to put others at ease? It's likely in the way you speak with them: non-confrontational, less hurried, spending a bit more time with small talk. It could be in the way you set up the room: observing hierarchy in the seating arrangement, utilizing props such as name tents and product design displays.

Nemawashi: **Groundwork (Literally, Binding Up the Roots for Transplant)**

This refers to the process of consensus building to make decisions through preliminary meetings and confidential one-on-one consultations. The actual meeting of a decision-making group, therefore, should harbor no surprises and may in fact be a kind of rubber-stamp ritual.

High-level Western executives have often asked, "Why do we need meetings before and after the actual meeting?" This strikes them as redundant. Yet for Japanese it is important to plant the seed of an idea in another person's mind and allow it to grow. This prevents blind-siding, catching someone off guard and big surprises in group meetings. *Nemawashi*, therefore, can be seen as a tool to preserve relationships and save face.

TIP: Don't expect to brainstorm or hash out problems with your Japanese partners during group meetings. Instead, be willing to incorporate *nemawashi* into your trans-Pacific decision-making processes. The increased time commitment to float an idea with more than one key figure in an organization should even be reflected in your business plan.

TIP: Brainstorming—think creatively about how to use written brainstorming as a starting point, prior to asking everyone to contribute ideas to the group.

Tateshakai: **Vertical Society**

Hierarchy, or status, is a key value in Japan, contributing to social stability in a densely populated country. This top-down relationship structure stems from Confucianism, which specified five key social relationships: lord and retainer, parent and child, older and younger siblings, husband and wife, and friend and friend. People of higher status are responsible for taking care of those below. In turn, those of lower status show due respect to their seniors. That mindset persists even in modern Japan, where one's relative status in the hierarchy determines the very language to be used in an interaction. Without that knowledge, therefore, communication can be difficult, even risky. This is why business-card exchange is critical at the beginning of a business relationship.

Hierarchy in modern Japan is not some kind of tyranny, in which lower-ranking individuals are worse off than the upper echelons. Most Japanese today identify themselves as middle class. Hence, their relative roles in the hierarchy are subtle, most determined by merit and effort, only a few still by birthright or location. One's university might be an important determinant in building your career network, for example. Japanese appear comfortable knowing their relative roles.

Here are some examples of how the hierarchy works in Japanese society at large:

- Referring to one's coworker as *sempai* (senior) or *kohai* (junior), according to the year of entry into the company or age, even if the difference is less than a year: This shows respect and is perfectly natural to most Japanese. *Sempai* often take on an unofficial mentoring role to their *kohai*.

- Order of speaking in a meeting and established roles of attendees: Japanese companies are generally organized according to the hierarchy, and it is virtually always clear who should speak first and who is responsible for which area. It might not be necessary to reiterate action items or to delegate specifically at the end of a meeting: it's "common sense."

- Emphasis on ranking throughout the educational process: lists of students' names are usually posted according to class ranking. Schools themselves are ranked, even at the high school level. Education is the principal way to raise one's relative status. Everyone knows the top five universities in Japan. Name-brand companies recruit exclusively from those schools.

- Seniority system in Japanese companies: While the seniority system remains intact, especially in the informal organization, the system has gradually been giving way to include merit-based evaluation and promotion. Note that this has not been an easy transition. For example, a well-known Japanese electronics company became a trendsetter in moving to a merit-based promotion system by promoting "younger" employees in their forties to *bucho*, or general manager; however, even after a decade this move is still causing some confusion and awkwardness, as the younger employees struggle to find new ways to communicate with and relate to their "seniors" who are now their subordinates. As for the older employees who are now subordinates, they put up with their

Changing Job Market

Note that given the increasing incidence of mid-career job transition in Japan, along with increasing numbers of contract employees, rank and experience might trump age in determining hierarchy.

younger bosses, knowing it might be for the good of the company.

- Size and relative value of gifts, wining and dining: this correlates to the giver's status. This is why it is important for VIP visitors to carefully evaluate the reputation and atmosphere of hotels and restaurants they use so as not to inadvertently damage corporate image.
- Asking questions to ascertain a person's age or other key background clues: When a Japanese knows, for example, that a colleague or associate graduated from his alma mater, a connection—even a special bond—is easily established. This can be regarded as more than just a coincidence; it's almost a matter of fate. Even attending the same high school, especially if it's a high-ranking one, will create a bond.
- One's university can still influence one's career path. Being connected with top-ranking Tokyo University, for example, confers instant status.

TIP: Don't be put off by questions asked to get at your status, such as age, position, or where you went to school. When meeting with Japanese customers for the first time, find out their relative status from your Japanese colleagues. In addition, always seek more background information, such as where they went to school, whether the schools are difficult to get into, and what they are known for. This information can help you show due respect when interacting with customers and will be useful as you build and maintain relationships with them. Some of our internationally experienced Japanese clients have paradoxically pointed out that while Japan is a hierarchical society, the gap between the highest and lowest isn't as wide as in other countries. For example, a Japanese CEO's compensation equals approximately sixteen times that of an average worker, whereas in the U.S., that number can be more than a thousand times.

型 *Kata*: Form

Kata refers to the way one presents oneself, to how a task is carried out, how a message is communicated, or how a duty is performed. *Kata* is a term taken from Japanese martial arts, meaning a set series of movements that prepare one to meet an opponent. In business, *kata* involves a prescribed or proper way of doing things, such as how to exchange business cards. For Japanese, *kata* constitutes a necessary buffer against surprise, a mechanism for creating an atmosphere that is predictable and therefore comfortable for everyone.

Following *kata* does not mean that Japanese are mere conformists. Japanese are just as different from one another as Westerners, though their brand of individualism might be expressed in more subtle ways. Through their collective socialization, however, the Japanese tend to be aware of a "right way" of doing things. Numerous books, including new-hire training manuals, are dedicated to the explanation of these proper forms. Using proper *kata* is considered respectable and even moral. A non-Japanese correctly using *kata* will be duly noted by Japanese and might even elicit rare praise and appreciation.

Update

We recently asked a number of Japanese executives about merit vs. seniority and hierarchical relationships. What we discovered was that the "old style" hierarchical tradition was still in place, alongside the meritocracy system. So even though meritocracy is becoming more common, it's still a system that is only tolerated, rather than embraced.

Below are some examples of how *kata* is practiced:

- Exchange of business cards.
- Giving and receiving gifts.
- Opening speeches or toasts at formal events.
- Highly structured schedules.
- At Shinto shrines: Visitors tossing a coin into the box, clapping twice, and bowing.
- At department stores: Uniformed clerks greeting customers with a bow; proper demeanor by department-store greeters.
- At gas stations: The process of greeting the customer loudly, cleaning the windshields with vigor, and risking life and limb to stop traffic so the driver can safely return to the street.
- New Year's greeting cards all arriving on January 1 all over Japan.
- New hires starting jobs on the first Monday in April—all wearing almost uniform black or navy blue suits. (Remember, just a few weeks before, these new hires were the same college kids who might have been sporting the Goth look, spiky green hair, or funky platform shoes.)

As a businessperson in Japan, you will not be expected to understand and follow to a tee all the subtleties of *kata*. However, it is important to keep on your toes more than you might elsewhere and note the way activities around you are carried out. Effort counts. To the degree that you are willing and able to learn proper greetings, business-card exchange, decorum for meetings, and the art of business entertaining, you will gain that much more respect from your Japanese counterparts.

The consequences of not understanding what is behind *kata* are:

- Japanese may seem dishonest or insincere.
- Japanese may seem rigid, inflexible, and overly formal.
- You may inadvertently communicate a lack of respect.
- You may seem less than trustworthy.
- You may embarrass your Japanese colleagues.
- You may feel discomfort when you stick out.
- You may be perceived as not demonstrating *doryoku*, or effort.

TIP: When giving direction to a Japanese employee, especially if you are in a leadership role, it's best to give more detail and some kind of format or protocol about how to carry out a project and not just leave it to them to figure out. Provide them with a *kata*: they are concerned not just about the results of the project but also about doing it the right way.

Business Example of *Ma*

When the top U.S. and Japanese executives of a joint venture were meeting to discuss a particularly difficult business situation, the CEO forcefully asked the group, "So, what are we going to do about this situation?" The ensuing pause was, from an American perspective, deadly a full minute before anybody had the guts to speak up. After the meeting, when the Japanese VP was asked about his take on the pregnant pause, he replied: "Silence? I didn't notice any silence." What seemed like an eternity to the Americans was for the Japanese merely the minimum required pause time.

場 *Ba*: Place

Ba refers to the location, surroundings, and the atmosphere a place creates. Changing the *ba* allows Japanese to modify their behavior. In the West we value being "yourself" wherever you are—consistency is important. In Japan, on the other hand, the same guy sitting next to you in a formal meeting with a rigid posture might loosen up after hours, sing Frank Sinatra, and become one of the silliest comics you've ever encountered. And, most important, he might disagree completely with what he had earlier agreed to in the meeting. The transition can be startling. The next day at work, it's back to business as usual. While the business conducted last night may be carried forward, most acts of impropriety are forgiven and forgotten as if they never happened.

TIP: When tensions mount in negotiations, for example, changing the *ba* can break up the flow and put everyone at ease. Japanese may appreciate the opportunity to associate informally outside the negotiating room. This allows them to speak more candidly.

間 *Ma*: Pause/Silence

Ma means an interval or a pause, like the space between words and sentences. Using *ma* allows time for others to consider the statement or question and formulate a thoughtful response. Pauses and silence are an integral part of conversations between two Japanese, who appreciate time to think in silence. In the West, and especially in the U.S., we are always talking; studies reveal that even as little as 3.5 seconds of silence between U.S. speakers creates discomfort. So we fill the gap with words. In Japan, an uncomfortable pause is more like twenty seconds. While we might pay lip service to the expression, "Silence is golden," Japanese actually believe it.

TIP: Practice reflective listening. Hold your quick answers in abeyance. Instead, demonstrate patience and sincere effort to understand what Japanese are saying by taking time to listen and pausing, in silence, to reflect. When asking questions, allow for adequate *ma*.

Wa: Harmony/Appearance of Harmony

Wa means harmony and refers to peace and tranquility in human relationships. It is said that *wa* provided the foundation of Japan's imperial system. In that sense, it is the most deeply rooted, longest-lived value in Japanese culture. *Kata* and the other behavioral practices discussed in this section can all be considered tools to maintain, if not absolute harmony, the appearance of harmony.

Here are some examples in business and social settings where you will see *wa*:

- Apologizing even if you are not directly to blame.
- Avoidance of overt disagreement in a meeting, even if it seems obvious that both sides' opinions are far apart. One might even go so far as to say "Yes" when one really means "No."
- Professional baseball teams, in certain situations, ending games in a tie.
- Ordering the same food as other people in one's group.
- Trying all the food that was ordered for you, even if you are squeamish about trying some of the items.
- Changing the meaning of a sentence at the end after seeing the facial expressions of the audience. (In the Japanese language, one can even negate the meaning of an entire sentence by varying the ending.)

TIP: Watch your facial expressions—try to keep your feelings to yourself and generally go with the flow.

ADVANCED TIP: Subjugate your own opinions and desires if they go against the overall harmony of the group. This is considered appropriate and even noble.

本
音
／
建
前

Honne/Tatemae: **Real Feeling/Public Position**

Western business executives frequently complain about this split between public and private views. A typical situation might involve a multi–site tele-conference involving Japan subsidiary colleagues, Japanese customers, and U.S. factory people. In the meeting the customer says the unit in question has no problems (*tatemae*), but later tells the real story (*honne*) to your Japan subsidiary colleague. This leaves the U.S. side baffled about the lack of openness in the original meeting. But the Japanese regard the meeting as the *ba* for *tatemae*, the public comments that will maintain the harmony and integrity of the various relationships. Balancing this is *honne*, one's real feeling or true intention, which, whether hidden or obvious, is not stated in a public situation; the *ba* for divulging *honne* is off-site, often in a bar or restaurant. In Japanese business, the skill of using *honne* and *tatemae* is a matter of course. It shows the mature businessperson's ability to finesse the situation and emerge without embarrassment or loss of face.

The following example illustrates how easy it is to misinterpret the importance and meaning of *tatemae* and *honne*: The American president of his company's Japan subsidiary heard about the two Japanese concepts and concluded that a policy eliminating *tatemae* in favor of *honne* would improve internal communication, create a more open atmosphere, and produce better results. The policy completely backfired, because it didn't make any sense to the Japanese employees. Assessing how to say something depending on the situation is a deeply rooted behavior in Japan that is necessary to preserve a harmonious environment. A good contrasting comparison might be to imagine suddenly asking your American colleagues to stop offering their opinions in order to avoid conflicts. It would be simply unnatural.

Examples of *honne/tatemae* in Japanese society:

- Not telling a patient that he or she is terminally ill (many patients actually prefer this).
- Not giving negative feedback to non-Japanese counterparts even when asked.
- Tendency among Japanese to "pretend" to understand English rather than interrupting and asking questions for clarification.
- Saying "It's difficult" when it's actually impossible.
- Laughing at jokes even when they don't understand them at all.
- Maintaining a pleasant smile or even laughing when explaining a tragic situation, such as the death of a family member.

From the Trenches

A morning business meeting in Japan was approaching 1 p.m., when the Japanese hosts suggested: "You must be hungry. Shall we order some lunch?" The Americans, too engrossed in the work to want a break just then, replied: "No, no. We had a late breakfast. We're OK." It didn't register with the Americans that the Japanese, who had been working since 6 a.m. that morning without a break, on top of their lengthy commutes to work, were themselves hungry and needed lunch. The Japanese did not make their real wishes known and continued the business meeting without a break.

Most cultures practice a version of *tatemae*—for example, telling the so-called "little white lie" in situations where it's not that important to be perfectly honest. Examples would be: "Gee, nice haircut" (even when you actually think it's dreadful), or "I'll get back to you as soon as possible" (even when you have little intention of doing so).

Awase: Adjusting to Fit In

合
わ
せ
This refers to the Japanese proclivity to fit in or to harmonize with the group or the situation. In business, it means downplaying one's individual opinion and preferences and deferring to the group or one's counterpart so as to be in alignment. *Awase* comes into play in major business dealings, for example, when a supplier attempts to anticipate its key customer's preferences by adding features to a product before they've even been requested by the customer. It can also come up in everyday situations, such as in deciding where to have lunch by soliciting opinions from everyone going. All this jockeying for a final decision may seem like a waste of time to many Westerners—"Why can't somebody just decide?" It qualifies as yet another example of the Japanese saying: "The nail that sticks up gets hammered down."

TIP: Don't always be the first to initiate decisions on what to do, where to go, or what to eat. Restrain your natural desire to be the leader or initiative taker. Force yourself to ask for opinions before giving them freely. Then practice *ma* (pause) before answering.

Spiritual Influences

Someone once observed that 130 percent of the population in Japan practices religion. What this means is that most people practice more than one religion. The two major religions in Japan are Shintoism and Buddhism. Nearly all Japanese consider themselves Buddhist, Shinto, or both and tend to follow the respective customs and rituals, particularly on formal occasions. Even so, very few Japanese consider themselves religious or particularly spiritual. The practices of the two religions simply shape a traditional way of life.

神道 Shintoism

Shinto is more a way of living or set of rituals than a conventionally understood religion. It represents an indigenous collection of beliefs and practices that define the character of Japan and have become symbols of the culture: the distinctively reddish-orange *torii* gates (sometimes varying in color) standing at the entrance of shrines; small amulets dangling from the windshield inside cars; *kami-dana*, or "god-shelves" (small shrines) in homes and offices containing special offerings, such as arrows, food, and other symbolic or protective items. Shintoism views evil as external impurity or disharmony with the natural order. An animistic religion, Shintoism speaks of eight million *kami*, or divinities, which permeate natural phenomena. Purity comes from harmony between humanity and these divinities. Many of Japan's time-honored rituals emerge from Shinto practice and mark important transitions in one's life: coming of age, graduation, opening a new store, building a home, weddings, etc.

KEY CONCEPTS WITH SHINTO ROOTS

Concept	Definition	Examples
WA	Harmony/Appearance of harmony	• Not contradicting someone in a meeting or gathering • Aplogize even if you are not directly to blame
KATA	The proper way/ The prescribed way	• Exchanging business cards • Doing ritual warm-up exercises before practicing martial arts

仏教 Buddhism

Buddhism came to Japan from India via China and Korea. It outlines an eight-fold path toward enlightenment, based on giving up all earthly desires. There are many different sects of Buddhism in Japan from the very ascetic to the most materialistic. Zen Buddhism is particularly prevalent in Japanese society, involving the practice of silent meditation and simplicity. An important Buddist principle is emptiness, "Emptiness is all, all is emptiness," emptying one's mind to find inner peace and knowledge, to forgo all desires. Less is more.

KEY CONCEPTS WITH BUDDHIST ROOTS

Concept	Definition	Examples
MA	Space/Pause/Silence	• A pause in conversation • Silent contemplation • A break in heated negotiation • The "empty spaces" in a Japanese garden
MU	Non-ego/ Reciprocity	• Building relationships before getting down to business • Asking someone else's opion first

Confucianism

This is a code of ethics or social behavior, rather than a religious doctrine, which came into Japan from China by way of Korea. Confucianism stressed the importance of fulfilling proper social roles and the resultant relationships of individuals in the family, neighborhood, workplace, and state, and the proper behaviors expected under various situations. (For more examples, see section on *tateshakai*, pages 132–36.) In short, Confucianism codified the hierarchical nature of those relationships; if the hierarchies were in proper balance, society would be harmonious.

KEY CONCEPTS WITH CONFUCIAN ROOTS

Concept	Definition	Examples
BON	Hierarchy/Vertical division	• Understanding one's role in a given situatuation • Shifting your speaking syle in accordance with a given situation
BA	Situation/Place	• Suggesting a break when tensions mount • Saving a controversial opinion for after hours in order to save face

The Reality about Common Sense

 Joshiki: Common Sense

What we might assume to be universal common sense actually varies according to cultural context. This can be very disconcerting. The goal of this chapter summary is to highlight a few so-called "common sense" assumptions you may be making. Depending on one's culture, the common-sense notions listed in the following chart can either be admired and respected or seen as childish, rude, or simply annoying. Looking at the chart, which side of the spectrum rings more true for you?

COMMON SENSE COMPARISON

Typical U.S. Concepts	Typical Japanese Concepts
Time is money.	Relationship is money.
If at first you don't succeed, try, try again.	Failure is shame.
If there is a will, there's a way.	*Shikata ga nai* (It can't be helped.)
Shoot first, ask quesions later.	Get it right the first time.
The squeaky wheel gets the grease.	The nail that sticks up gets hammered down.
Lay your cards on the table.	Silence is golden.
Get it in writing; say what you mean; don't put words in my mouth.	*Haragei* ("belly talk," or gut feeling); *Ishin denshin* (intuitively reading each other's hearts).
Get to the point.	Hear one, understand ten.
Don't take no for an answer.	Unlike the oak, the bamboo that bends does not get blown down.
The self-made man; do it your-self; you can only depend on yourself.	Seek shelter in the shade of a big tree; one-man sumo wres-tling (futility of effort without group support).
Play it by ear; wing it; think on your feet.	Polish one's arms (master something through great effort and experience over time).
Don't just stand there, do something; just do it.	Sitting on a stone for three years (endurance is a virtue).
My rights as an individual.	The importance of the group.
"We are taking every possible action."	"It's under investigation."
A rolling stone gathers no moss (don't get weighted down, keep moving).	A rolling stone gathers no moss (it takes time to aquire status).
I am not a typical American.	I am a typical Japanese.

CHAPTER 4

Communication in Action

So-Called "Soft Skills" That Get Hard Results

In the age of globalization, communication is emerging as *the* pivotal issue. In the Internet age, we have the technology to communicate instantaneously around the planet, but do we have the human-to-human skill set to maximize the effectiveness and productivity of those communication tools? In the previous chapter we considered effective business strategies in Japan, but they are only part of the total picture of success. Communication issues play an equally critical role in completing the picture. In short, business strategies and communication issues are two sides of the same partnership-building coin. For example, learning how to modify your speaking is critical for building relationships and establishing proper credibility. Unless you happen to speak fluent business Japanese, you will need to understand how to use the English language in a more constructive way when working with Japan. This section deals with the critical issues and preferred methods of communicating with Japanese.

Only in recent years has the business world included communication among the make-or-break organizational success factors. Communication barriers can be the bane even of monocultural business interactions. When you factor in cultural differences, business interactions can become even more exasperating, stressful, even dangerous, and sometimes downright hilarious.

Influences on Japanese Communication Style

While not without basis, these top ten stereotypical complaints are repeatedly lodged, particularly by inexperienced businesspeople, about communicating with Japanese:

1. They don't speak up in meetings, especially when the news is bad.
2. They don't voice their opinions.
3. They cave in instead of providing a solid argument for their position.
4. They are stone-faced—I can't read them.
5. Even when they don't understand, they don't ask for clarification.
6. They say "Yes" when they mean "No."
7. I can't get a straight answer from them—how can I be sure that their answer is really a "Yes"?
8. They take a long time to get to the point.

9. Why don't they just relax?
10. They don't speak English very well. (Note: Japanese tend to rank English as their number one problem in doing business internationally.)

A Point about Communication and Context

Why do we perceive the Japanese in the ways listed above? While people in Western countries tend to rely on explicit information, Japanese people tend to rely on contextual clues in communication as much as on the words or content of any message. There's a famous expression in Japan: "Hear one, understand ten." For the Japanese, this expression means that a mature and sophisticated listener would be able to glean the speaker's true intention, plus multiple nuances, based as much on nonverbal contextual clues—such as place, dress, status, intonation, facial expression, and posture—as from the actual words.

In this sense, Japan is often referred to as a "high-context" culture, where considerable time is invested in establishing the broad parameters of what is at issue in an interaction before addressing the issue directly. In "low-context" cultures, by contrast, little time is invested in broad parameters; they are developed only if absolutely needed. A low-context culture, then, cuts to the chase and takes a more direct approach to communication: "Tell it like it is," "Say what you mean," or "Don't put words in my mouth." In low-context cultures, where content is seen as more important than context, "Yes" tends to mean "Yes" and even "Yes, I agree." On the other hand, in high-context cultures like Japan, a "Yes" might have several possibilities depending on the situation, such as "I hear what you are saying," but rarely indicates outright agreement. Later in this chapter we will give some important hints about how to decipher "Yes" and "No."

Common Communication Gaps: English in Japan

Yes, you too need to learn how to speak English as a second language.

In case you haven't had this confirmed already, the language of global business today is English. English as a second language (ESL) is the single most popular subject in the world after mathematics. Indeed, about ⅓ of the world's population speak some form of English (two billion people), making it the most widely used language on the planet. Effective use of ESL—often characterized by slower speech, using fewer and more efficient words, reducing idiomatic phrases and slang—is paramount to getting something accomplished and achieving mutual understanding in a global business setting.

As in so many countries, English is taught in schools throughout Japan. The key difference in Japan is that the English-language curriculum focuses on the universally required entrance exam for getting into a good university, which, in turn, is a requirement for getting into a good company and being set for life. The study of English, therefore, is less about functional communication in a foreign language than about avoiding mistakes on that exam. Your counterparts could probably diagram a sentence or conjugate a verb, but if they break into a cold sweat when dealing with you in English, it could be that they are reliving the pressure of their childhood education all over again.

English is required of all Japanese for the six years of junior high and high school, and more recently has been instated at the elementary school level. The instructional emphasis is on rote memorization, analysis of often-obscure grammatical points, and written translation—mostly calculated for passing the university entrance exam. That approach has left Japan, along with communist North Korea, at the bottom of the TOEFL (Test of English as a Foreign Language) achievement tests in English among twenty-five Asian nations. Japanese kids actually memorize voluminous vocabulary lists and numberless sentence patterns to pass their tests but may have had few chances to actually utter a coherent sentence in conversation. This is a handicap that seriously hinders Japanese in their global business endeavors.

In recent years, there has been an upsurge in Japan for learning English. In the heady bubble years of the 1980s, English conversation was all the rage but mostly as a light hobby or status symbol. Hundreds of "English Conversation Lounges" and fly-by-night schools popped up, featuring as instructors virtually anyone looking vaguely foreign wanting to make a quick yen—blondes were at a premium. In response to internationalization pressures in the late '80s the Japanese government launched the Japan English Teachers (JET) program to bring more native English speakers into the Japanese classroom. Today there are over 5,500 such teachers on the ground in junior high and high schools across the country. In early

> **Scenario**
>
> You are hosting a Japanese delegation. The Japan side brings along its own interpreter to assist the Japanese higher ups, and you know full well that the big boss really does speak English pretty well . . . so what is he up to? Why doesn't he just use the English that he knows? Chances are he is just saving his own face (not looking foolish speaking in English) or saving you from the trouble of having to listen to his broken English. The interpreter a convenience that works well for them.

2000, then–Prime Minister Keizo Obuchi proposed that English become Japan's official second language in order to accelerate the pace of globalization. English is just now starting to be taught at the elementary school level, and eager parents are enrolling their toddlers in English-focused preschools. NHK, the BBC of Japan, now makes it a requirement that its newscasters speak English. The current English boom has more to do with business survival skills. The types of schools popping up now are aggressive, professionally run businesses, hiring certified language instructors. Some of the larger foreign companies in Japan are all but requiring an overseas degree.

So does this all mean we are in the clear and our communication problems will be solved? Hardly.

How many of us are really comfortable doing business or even conversing in a second language? Bravo if your answer is "Yes." When you hear others speaking in an unfamiliar language, do you feel uncomfortable or right at home? Consider the last time you needed to communicate with someone whose English was lacking, say in a service situation. How well did you do—was it a successful and pleasant interaction?

While there may be a coterie of newly minted, fluent speakers of English in Japan, anyone over thirty might have had limited exposure to using "real" English until well into his or her career. Also, speaking English fluently doesn't necessarily reflect one's level of competence on the job. This has been an embarrassing lesson for some international companies in Japan; they have promoted local employees based solely on English ability, only to find that those employees fall flat due to a lack of hard business skills. The highly qualified manager or engineer, with whom you really need to talk about your joint product development, might have hated anything to do with studying English and be unable to use it as a result. That makes doing business in Japan a little more complicated, but it is a pervasive reality. It's not a bad idea once in a while to show your appreciation for how well your Japanese colleagues use the English that they do know. Certainly they would encourage any efforts you might show to communicate in Japanese.

In addition, non-Japanese need to be aware that fluent English speakers are usually still culturally Japanese. That is, they probably won't know most English colloquialisms or idioms, and their communication style is still very Japanese. In short, their thinking is still different. They might, for example,

> **Essential Tip**
> Never assume shared understanding, until all action steps or agreements have been *absolutely confirmed*. International businesspeople need to consistently use good strategies for communication, whatever the perceived level of their Japanese colleagues' English ability. *This may be the most critical piece of advice in this entire book.*

struggle with persuasive point-by-point presentations or in making convincing justifications for proposals. They might not be comfortable saying "No" directly.

Hierarchical Influences on Japanese Communication Style

Japanese live in a vertical world, or *tateshakai*, often cited as a legacy of Confucianism, a school of thinking imported from China in the sixteenth century, which celebrates adherence to one's role and respective place (or rank) in society. When Japanese encounter each other, a matrix of criteria kicks in to determine who is senior or junior in relation to whom (see *tateshakai* diagram below).

This hierarchy then dictates the manner of one's speech, including choice of vocabulary and level of politeness. In contrast, many Westerners reserve the right to disregard any perceived hierarchy and bring everyone to the same level.

EXAMPLES OF *TATESHAKAI* RELATIONS

Older	Teacher	Parent Company	Customer	Doctor	Engineer	Big name school
↕	↕	↕	↕	↕	↕	↕
Younger	Student	Branch Office	Supplier	Patient	Non-engineer	Less famous school

Japanese take comfort in knowing where they fit into the grand hierarchical scheme. Unlike some more traditional societies, however, Japanese can move about in the hierarchy most prominently by getting into a top university or joining the right company. Further, hierarchies are relative: you may be near the top in one situation but at the lower end in another. In a Japanese organization, one's position in the hierarchy is usually determined by age and/or the year one entered the company. As mentioned in the previous chapter, the *sempai* (one's senior) has an unspoken responsibility to "take care of" his or her *kohai* (one's junior), to show them the ropes, help them build their relationship network, secure opportunities, and so on. While similar to mentoring, it's not necessarily voluntary. The *kohai* in turn must show respect to the *sempai* and assist the *sempai* in any way possible. Note that the age difference may be very slight, and these days, one's *sempai* may be younger but in a higher position. One's position in the hierarchy affects the way one speaks Japanese, especially in determining the proper level of politeness and sometimes how direct one can be.

155

Even when speaking English, Japanese are obsessed with using polite language. So they may hesitate to speak in English at all, out of fear that they won't be showing the listener proper respect.

Was That a "Yes" or a "No"?

Taking into account the highly contextual nature of Japanese language and communication, the understood hierarchy, the cultural norms such as harmony, adjusting to fit in, and other aspects of human relationships, you may by now be able to predict why it might be difficult for Japanese to come out and just say "No!" As in any other culture, Japanese people most certainly have ways of saying "No." It's a matter of reading between the lines and picking up on the cues not directly spoken. This next list provides you with some of those key cues.

Deciphering "No"/Checking for "Yes"

It's time to worry when:

- Your Japanese counterpart sucks in air through his/her teeth.
- Your counterpart scratches the back of his/her head, especially if he/she grimaces.
- Your counterpart tilts his/her head with knitted brow.
- Your counterpart doesn't ask any questions, even when given plenty of time to do so.

Or, it's not a good sign when your counterpart says:

- (Silence)
- "There are a few difficulties . . . "
- "It's difficult . . . "
- "We will investigate . . . "

- "It's under investigation . . . "
- "We will consider it . . . "

How to Check for Agreement/ Understanding/ Getting Feedback

- Talk about specific timelines and deadlines, and get their response.
- Call on people by name to ensure orderly turn taking and clear understanding.
- Summarize agreements, confirm alignment, and then send a confirmation e-mail afterward.
- Have them summarize for you: "Could you summarize your understanding of what we've agreed to?"

Possible Interpretations for No Response to E-mail

- They are avoiding saying a direct "No."
- The *nemawashi* process is in operation—complete answer to come.
- They didn't receive your e-mail.
- They didn't catch the urgency required.
- They are still trying to translate it into Japanese and back into English.
- The appropriate person to respond is currently unavailable.
- There are roadblocks to responding—possible loss of face.
- They don't know who you are or what your role is and are trying to figure out the best way to respond, or are simply setting your message aside for the time being.

A Real "Yes" Might Come in the Form Of . . . (With Japanese Translations)

- "I'll do my best" (*Gambarimasu*).

- "We will do our best" (*Gambarimasu/Gambari-masho*).

- "We" (In a "we" culture, this implies more responsibility/accountability than "I").

- "We will try" (*Yatte mimasu*).

- "Let's try" (*So shimasho*).

The English-Language Challenge in Japan

The population of Japan is among the most educated in the world—even the homeless are avid readers. The biggest failure in education, however, has been in the area of foreign-language instruction, which emphasizes rote memorization of sentence patterns. Fear of failing to be perfect severely inhibits oral language usage. Written skills are usually better—when in doubt, write it down. Typically, Japanese feel they cannot master spoken English and tend to blame all intercultural miscommunication on "my poor English." The intrinsic structure of the Japanese language presents a further challenge when Japanese take on English. The subject of a Japanese sentence is often omitted and the verb is always at the end. This means that the key information, usually contained in the verb, comes at the end of the sentence. Westerners who expect the key information up front, often interrupt their Japanese counterparts before they can finish their sentences. Japanese find this very frustrating.

Typical Errors That Japanese Make in English

- Overly polite language: Japanese are nearly obsessed about using the polite language patterns

learned in school, which may be archaic and out
of place with native speakers of English.

- Overly direct language: For example, overusing
"must," "have to," and "had better." Many Japanese know they need to be more direct in English, and they assume that the imperative form is
the way to go. They were taught that "had better" is a polite suggestion.

  "You had better go to Kyoto for sight seeing."
  "You have to see a doctor."

- Use of questions stated in the negative when at-
tempting to be polite: In Japanese, the negative
is considered less direct and more polite.

  "Don't you want coffee?"
  "Why don't you give me that report?"

- Wrong answer to negative questions: In Japanese
the answer is the opposite.

  Q: "You didn't see him yesterday?"
  A: "Yes, (I didn't see him)."

- Mixing up "he" and "she": In Japanese, not only
is the gender-specific pronoun often dropped,
many Japanese have a hard time distinguishing
between the initial consonant sounds "h" and
"sh."

- Large numbers: The numbering system is very
different in Japanese. For example, ten thousand
becomes "one (unit of) ten thousand" (*ichi man*).
Japanese may need time to translate to get the
correct number when speaking. Written numbers don't pose such a problem.

- Misuse of "almost" and "mostly": There's only
one word in Japanese to convey both meanings.

  "We almost closed the sale with the cus-

159

tomer." (This means: "It's pretty much done, we expect to close soon," as opposed to "We came close but didn't succeed.")

"We are almost men." (Should be: "We are mostly men.")

- Use of "maybe" or "I think": Japanese tend to use these as speech softeners to make their statement more respectful, but this could send a conflicting message to the listener.

"We can get it by tomorrow . . . I think."

"I agree with what you have proposed today . . . maybe."

Characteristics of a Good Japanese Listener

What do we assume to be good listening behavior? Note that the behaviors below would be considered ideal or polite, particularly in a more formal situation, to show respect to someone of a higher rank. Most of them demonstrate the need to maintain the appearance of harmony. Same-company situations, particularly in the high-tech world, would be more direct, less deferential.

VERBAL TRAITS

- Does not interrupt the speaker.
- Pretends to understand minor, unclear points.
- Might nod and say "*Hai*" (Yes) to indicate listening concentration.
- Waits until the speaker is finished before clarifying or asking questions.
- Might wait until afterward, and ask another listener to clarify.
- Does not point out careless mistakes of the speaker or directly disagree.
- Does not leave the room until the speaker is finished.

NONVERBAL TRAITS

- Maintains erect posture (*kincho suru*—literally, "Be nervous").
- Maintains a "pleasant" expression.
- Gives "listening feedback" (*aizuchi*).
- Nods, and might say "*Hai*," "*Eh*," or "*Uhn*" to indicate that he/she is present and listening. When the conversation is in English, this response usually comes out as "Yes," but it usually implies "Yes, I'm listening," and does not necessarily indicate agreement or understanding.

MINDSET

- Reads between the lines: context is key.

Meeting Each Other Halfway

Relearning How to Speak English

In this section we will see that whatever the perceived communication gap, the responsibility for bridging it lies equally on both sides. If we're to be better understood, we have to start speaking English in a way that helps Japanese understand us. The tourist stereotype is that one need only speak louder to the non-native speaker in order to be understood. What we'd like to present here is a list of proven strategies that facilitate smooth communication (and don't insult the listener). This preparation may be the most crucial and challenging that you undertake before heading to Japan.

Asking for Repetition . . . Again

"When I don't understand something that my Japanese counterpart has said—maybe it's the accent or the sen-

PROVEN STRATEGIES FOR BETTER ENGLISH COMMUNICATION WITH JAPANESE

Strategy	Putting It into Practice
Simplify	Use short sentences and simple words.
Slow down and speak clearly	Speak slowly and clearly. Pause between phrases and sentences.
Write down numbers	Always write large numbers down, even if everyone is nodding in agreement. There is simply too much room for error here.
Take turns	Balance airtime—if you are doing all the talking, you may need to pause more frequently or direct a specific question to a specific person.
Allow for silent thinking time	Silence is considered normal in Japanese conversation. Especially after asking a difficult question, count to ten and allow others to think without rushing to fill the silence.
Facilitate	Use gestures, examples, written words, visual aids, charts, or numbers to illustrate points.
Check for understanding	Occasionally ask, "Am I being clear?" or "Does that make sense?" Avoid "Do you understand?" (The answer is always "Yes" even if they don't.)
Repeat key points	When asked to repeat, first repeat the same sentence exactly but more slowly. Then try rephrasing, if necessary.
Summarize and confirm	Summarize key points and ideas at the end of each agenda item and once again at the end of the meeting. Always summarize "same-side conversation" in teleconferences.
Understand feedback	Japanese might not interrupt to give feedback about their level of understanding. Learn to recognize subtle cues such as puzzled expressions, head tilt, long pauses, rising "Eh?" noises, and other ways of giving feedback.

peat before it becomes rude or not worth the effort?" It's certainly OK to ask your colleagues to repeat key points. Ask for an example. Have them draw a graphic representation of what they are trying to say. Take responsibility for any lack of understanding. In a teleconference, you can also fault the equipment. As a last resort you can ask someone else to summarize the point, all the while taking responsibility for not catching what's been said. In business you can't afford gaps in mutual understanding—go ahead and use the range of the above communication strategies now and avoid a potentially much bigger mess to clean up later.

"That Went Over Like a Lead Balloon" and Other Jokes: Language to Avoid

In your travels as a global businessperson, you have probably noticed not only that certain jokes don't travel well, but that idioms, colloquialisms, and slang often elicit glazed expressions on the faces of non–American counterparts. We certainly don't advocate eliminating use of shared humor in building relationships and melting the ice. It's important to remember that most people who speak English as a second language can only go so far to keep up with all of our linguistic idiosyncrasies and subtleties. If you can't avoid the following when speaking with Japanese colleagues, explanation may be required.

1. Subtle humor, especially sarcasm: "Oh, that's just great!" Without context, the meaning is lost.
2. Complex structures, questions within questions: "What I am trying to ask you is why didn't you inform us about this problem at the time of shipment?"
3. Either/or questions: They will probably hear only

one part of the question and you'll get an inaccurate or confusing answer, as in the following example:

Q : "Are we going to do a quick fix here, or find some longer term solution?"

A : "Yes."

4. Reductions and contractions: These are very difficult for Japanese to hear. Examples:

"going to" → "gonna"
"want to" → "wanna"
"did you" → "didja"
"cannot" → "can't"

5. Unusual starting phrases: "If that is the case, then . . . " "Should you happen to find a problem, then . . . " "You know the minutes I sent out last week?"

6. Difficult multisyllable vocabulary: "My overriding hypothesis is that the industrial unit is discombobulated over our tardiness."

7. Idiomatic language or slang: This can sound really odd to the Japanese ear. Examples: "That went over like a lead balloon"; "Can you give me some ballpark figures?"; "You're beating around the bush"; "Let's table the issue"; "Let's have a go at it."

8. If you catch yourself uttering an idiom (usually followed by puzzled looks) go ahead and explain it to your listeners. They will probably appreciate the impromptu English insight: "Well that was a no-brainer. . . . Oh, let me explain what I meant by that . . . " And don't be surprised if it shows up in subsequent communication from your Japan partners.

Strategies for Shifting Communication Style

Most of us can identify hair or suit styles, but how much time do we spend examining other people's communication styles? One's communication style often overrides the actual words in the message. In the chart on the next page we introduce some typical Western behaviors that might convey unintended messages.

This basic concept involves taking on communication behaviors and skills that are familiar to the target group. Effective style shifting cannot be learned overnight. The appropriate behaviors are indeed skills, like your golf swing or like playing the piano; it is therefore recommended to see these behaviors modeled, then to practice them consistently until they feel comfortable. We can also banish the notion frequently voiced (by Americans) that we will become "too Japanese" if we seriously make the effort to shift our communication style. No Japanese would ever regard you in this way nor expect you to change your identity or innate personality in any way.

In short, by gradually shifting your style in the direction of the arrows below, you can facilitate understanding and gain the respect of your counterparts.

Electronic Communication: E-mail, IM, Teleconferences, and Videoconferences

Whenever possible, meet face-to-face with your Japanese counterparts, particularly in the beginning stages of a team project or major launch. Any electronic alternative will very likely not give the same important connection-building platform, but is excellent for subsequent meetings and ongoing communications.

E-Mail, Instant Messaging (IM)

Remember that as convenient and globally instantaneous as e-mail is supposed to be, it is a very low-context transactional medium for communication, fraught with the potential to provide more opportunities for mis-

COMMON WESTERN BEHAVIORS AND THEIR UNINTENDED MESSAGES

Style	Common Behaviors	Possible Unintended Message
Assertive	• Use "I" a lot • Give a lot of ideas at once • Don't apologize	• Egocentric • Shallow • Immature • Arrogant
Analytical	• Ask "Why?" often • Demand proof with data • Show no interest in background or experience	• Impatient • Argumentative • Not "sincere"
Direct	• Get down to business quickly • Confront, raise "problems" to solve • Make sustained eye contact • Give direct opinions • Don't go through proper channels	• Impatient • Confrontational • Lacking consideration • Disrespectful
Informal	• Use relaxed posture at meetings • Use humor, jokes • Continue to use nicknames in formal situations	• Insincere, not hard-working • Not serious • Disrespectful
Specific	• Ask for yes/no answers, expect quick responses • "Protect" information, don't always provide background details	• Shallow • Pushy • Secretive
Verbal	• Talk a lot, don't allow silence • Push for answers	• Egocentric, controlling • Pushy

STRATEGIES FOR STYLE SHIFTING

Desired Shift in Style	Behaviors / Skills
From → **To** Assertive → Harmonious	• Count to 5 or 10 between sentences and questions • Use "we" instead of "I" • Be humble, apologetic, modest
Analytical → Intuitive	• Ask for background instead of just asking "Why?" • Consider relationships and reactions along with data
Direct → Indirect	• Create a positive, comfortable atmosphere • Draw out opinions of others before announcing a problem • Use less eye contact than usual • Ask for others' opinions first and listen
Informal → Formal	• Sit up straight, be more formal • Use the right protocol for the situation • Use surname + *san*
Specific → Broad	• Provide "nice-to-know" background information • Get others' ideas before reaching conclusions and asserting your own position
Verbal → Nonverbal	• Give space in the conversation, pause • Try to read nonverbal signals (air sucked between teeth, folded arms, tilted heads) • Tone down your own body language

1
2
3
4
5
6
7
8

communication. Here are some ideas on how to ensure greater success:

- Be formal and polite—if you are initiating the correspondence, begin with "Dear last name + *san*" (e.g., "Dear Yamaguchi-san" or "Hello, Yamaguchi-san").
- Begin with a brief greeting.
- Identify yourself and your group or project.
- Include adequate background detail regarding your request or situation.
- Be specific about what you need; don't expect them to make any assumptions or do any guesswork.
- Keep your message as brief and clear as possible.
- Enumerate your points or requests; use bullet points.
- Check your message carefully for idiomatic expressions, clarity, and adequate background information.
- If you don't get a response, follow up (politely) and assume responsibility for any misunderstanding or lack of clarity.

Teleconference, Videoconference, and Virtual-Meeting Best Practices

While teleconferences and virtual or Internet-based meetings might seem to be a step up from e-mail in terms of "live" communication, they are still very challenging for the Japanese audience. Whenever possible, choose video conferencing, as it gives your listeners more of the badly needed visual and contextual clues as to the intended message. The tips below are effective methods of facilitating this type of meeting to ensure effective communication across all cultures:

- Send the meeting agenda well in advance so people have time to formulate their responses. Try to resist the temptation to cram everything into one meeting. Prioritizing and reducing the agenda might actually lead to more productive teleconference meetings.

- Initiate the *nemawashi* or groundwork process in advance—it still applies to virtual meetings.

- Identify all who are present, and make sure everyone identifies him or herself when speaking.

- Be extra careful about turn-taking—allow for a few extra moments of pause between sentences and between two speakers. You may sometimes need to call on people by name for smoother entry into the conversation.

- Make sure everyone has the agenda and other supporting materials before the meeting. Make use of any written materials frequently during the meeting.

- In teleconferences, speakers need to remember to identify themselves, even if they have already spoken in the meeting.

- Always confirm and/or summarize what you've heard, and do this consistently. You will also be doing your counterparts a big favor.

- Keep your volume consistent, especially at the ends of sentences.

- Allow time for "sidebar" communication and confirmation in Japanese. As we mentioned in earlier chapters, this is a good way to ensure that everyone is on the same page.

- In a videoconference, make sure you are in view of the camera. Body language is important to

Japanese and can help them understand what you are saying.

- Confirm agreements/action steps at the end, and ask for their confirmation.
- Send a follow-up e-mail. Japanese are generally more comfortable with written rather than spoken communication. Sometimes follow-up phone calls to key individuals can also increase productivity in electronic meetings.

Even in a teleconference, be mindful that Japanese cultural norms in communication still apply. It may be difficult to "hash it out" to reach agreement. Don't expect a great deal of individual initiative taking—the need to have group consensus may still prevail. Even if major decisions aren't being made within the context of the teleconference, regular team-to-team communication is essential. Show patience and consistency in using "best practices" for teleconference meeting facilitation. Your efforts will be appreciated.

Interpreters

Having your own interpreter is one of the best insurance policies to ensure the success of your visit. Just as one would not sign a complex business contract without consulting an attorney, it's not smart to go into a bilingual situation without a good interpreter. You can try things on your own, but you increase your chances for miscommunication, conflict, and business failure. It's very likely that your Japanese counterparts will have their own interpreter. Many feel it's acceptable to rely on the other team's interpreter, but that can be risky. Guess where that interpreter's loyalties lie? Get your own interpreter.

Selecting a Good Interpreter

It's best to have someone you feel comfortable with and who can provide cultural interpretations of the non-verbal communication. Also, many business areas are so specialized that your interpreter really should have same-industry experience. Such persons can be hard to find, so get references. In all cases, you will still be responsible for preparing your interpreter for your specific industry, situation, and any accompanying jargon. If your company is contemplating hiring a Japanese person in hopes that they can also take on this role, be careful. It's far more important to hire someone who is highly qualified for the job. Really effective interpretation is a complex skill and an art—even perfectly bilingual people often don't have this skill. Also, because of the person's role or level in your company, it may not be appropriate for him or her to also fill in as interpreter. Sometimes the outside interpreter can have an advantage in being perceived as the "trusted third party."

Using an Interpreter

You need to brief your interpreter on your strategy, on what you hope to accomplish in the meeting, and how you intend to present your information. In addition, to familiarize the interpreter with your communication style, vocabulary, and turn of phrase, we strongly recommend a thorough dry run. You don't want any surprises during the actual meeting. Here are some other considerations:

- The meeting generally will take approximately 1.5 times longer than if it were a monolingual event. Plan accordingly. You are still likely to save time in the long run and get higher quality input.
- Interpretation for most business meetings is not

simultaneous but consecutive. This means you need to stop at frequent intervals, so that the interpreter, who will have been taking notes while you speak, can convey your message. You can practice this in the dry run.

- While the interpreter is speaking, it is best to focus your attention not on the interpreter but on your counterpart across the table and/or on the materials in front of you. Remember that the interpreter is present not as a strategist or decision maker but simply as a conduit for your thoughts. Try therefore to interact with the other team almost as if there were no interpreter. You need to be looking for the other side's responses, nonverbal reactions, and so on, in any case. Don't miss that opportunity by gazing at the interpreter. It is advisable, however, to glance quickly at the interpreter every now and then to make sure you are proceeding at a proper pace.

- Be vigilant about modifying your English, especially about slowing down. Chances are, your Japanese counterparts speak some English but can't take it at bullet speed. Also, avoid long stretches of monologue loaded with information. Keep comments brief. Simplify your vocabulary, and cut out idioms and jargon.

- Finally, use the interpreter to debrief your meetings. He or she can help you understand why certain aspects of the meeting went well or not so well and thereby contribute to your cultural understanding and help you prepare for the next interaction or meeting.

Case Study: Miscommunication in Meetings

The following case study is based on a composite of frequently heard complaints from actual meetings that went awry because of missed cultural cues and unstated assumptions. See if you can identify what went wrong and what might be done differently in the future to avoid "unproductive" meeting situations.

There are three parties in this teleconference meeting:

1. U.S. Company in Sacramento, California
2. Japan Subsidiary of the U.S. company, in Saitama
3. Japanese Customer in Tokyo

   U.S. Headquarters Representative: Justin
   Japan Subsidiary Representative: Morimoto

The Japanese Customer has encountered a problem, possibly a defect, with a new computer-related product purchased from the U.S. Company in Sacramento. The U.S. Company, in turn, provides the Japanese Customer with a particular, customized solution for their potential problem. The Japanese Customer wants to be sure the fix will work in all situations. The three parties hold a meeting, and Justin, the U.S. HQ representative, reassures the Japanese Customer and explains that the fix is more than adequate. An hour of this goes by, and after several rounds of explanation and Q and A, Justin hears the Japanese Customers saying, "*Hai, hai.*" It seems that no one has any further issues to bring up. His Japan Subsidiary representative, Morimoto-san, summarizes the meeting and brings it to a close. Justin is glad to have this issue resolved so he can make it to his next meeting.

Later that same day, Justin gets a desperate phone call from Morimoto-san explaining that the Japanese

Customers are completely dissatisfied with this solution. They don't believe that it will cover other usage situations and want to see more thorough data and root-cause analysis from the U.S. manufacturing division.

Issues

- Justin is thinking, "Why didn't they bring this up at the meeting?"
- Seems that the meeting was a waste of time.
- Frustration on both sides due to apparent gap in understanding.
- Apparent lack of openness on the part of the Japanese customer.
- Apparent lack of sincere customer concern on the part of the U.S. supplier.

What Happened?

The Japanese Customer operates in a high-context environment. It is unlikely that they would explain their thinking but would assume that the supplier would simply be perfectly willing to send them any related data, especially when there has been a product malfunction. Think zero defects—that's the Japanese benchmark. Japanese also assume that the customer is on a high level—"The customer is god," runs their proverb. So the customer should get whatever the customer requests.

Justin made the critical global business error of assuming mutual understanding. He really needs more clarification. With his low-context communication style, Justin expects to have issues raised directly. Justin was happy that the meeting came to a close due to his own time constraints, but he'll no doubt end up spending more time later following up with this customer request.

With his high-context communication style, Morimoto-san implicitly understood the context of the Japanese customer's issue and assumed that Justin would read between the lines, too, without further explanation.

TIP: Justin and Morimoto-san should send follow-up e-mails after the meeting to everyone concerned to confirm exactly what was requested and what was agreed upon.

Communication Strategies for Future Meetings

Assume responsibility for any miscommunication. Justin could start with a phrase like, "Perhaps something is missing from my explanation. It seems that we're not 100 percent statisfied."

Modify communication. Justin and his colleagues need to slow down and simplify their communication, especially when problems arise.

Clarify assumptions. Since it might not occur to Morimoto-san to explain in detail the background of the Japanese customer's complaint, it would help to ask him something like this: "Could you give us the customer's thinking on the relationship between the fix we've provided and their need for more data?"

Provide Context. It would also help for Justin to provide more background from his standpoint. Give the Japan side the context it needs to grasp the U.S. point of view.

Ask more open-ended questions. "What is (the customer's) point of view on the product performance?"

Facilitate. Especially when things are not progressing, Justin needs to stop and summarize his point of view or even review the process of the meeting itself: "We seem to be repeating the same point over and over rather than agreeing on the validity of this solution. May I ask you to help us understand the thinking behind your concern with this solution?"

When interacting with Japanese it is important to comprehend the nonverbal signals, rather than just listen for words. The challenge is to be aware of our assumptions and consistently clarify them. This means that, beyond modifying our usual communication patterns, we need to tune our radars to the often subtle cues sent by our Japanese counterparts.

The following is a composite of interviews with several Japanese engineers and managers in high-tech industries. The comments here tie together and reinforce many of the key points from this chapter on communication, and the previous chapter on business. Look for ways that you can improve your own approach to working with your Japanese counterparts.

1. What are some key points that your U.S. counterparts should understand about Japan and its business practices to work effectively with their Japanese customers and colleagues?

   Answer: Fear of failure is often a guiding motivational factor among Japanese. One hundred percent perfection is the desired state. Zero defects. Japanese are loath to launch a new product until it is perfected. There might not be a second chance.

2. What are the key communication style differences that Americans should be aware of and adjust to?

   Answer: Listening and speaking in meetings. In the U.S., all attendees, not just the one making a presentation, would expect to have input in a nonstop exchange of viewpoints. In Japan, by contrast, the one presenting would expect to speak to intent listeners, who would not interrupt. Questions and comments would come only at the end.

3. In meetings, what's the best way to handle sidebar communication in Japanese, and why does this happen so often?

   Answer: Ninety percent of the time the sidebar communication is simply for the Japanese side to confirm their understanding of the last thing you said, and it's generally very constructive. No need to panic about what might be going on. Exercise patience. If you sense a lack of understanding, ask if you need to offer any further clarification.

4. What is the best medium (phone/voicemail, e-mail/fax) for urgent communication? Non-urgent communication?

   Answer: For urgent communication and quick updates, a phone call is acceptable. However, to avoid miscommunication, Japanese would still prefer to have a message in writing. It's a good idea, therefore, to follow up all spoken communication—urgent or not with e-mail. In fact, e-mail is generally best, because it's easy to read and respond to without on-the-spot pressure.

5. What further communication advice do you have for your non-Japanese counterparts to help make communication in English go more smoothly?

   Answer: Slow down, so that your Japanese counterparts can follow the conversation and participate. Summarize key points as you proceed and confirm understanding. In teleconferences with Japanese customers, verify that the sound quality is good. Japanese might not tell you that the sound is muffled.

Understand the difficulty Japanese face when they must communicate in English. Show patience with their effort. Don't assume a correlation between English-speaking level and professional competence.

6. What should your U.S. counterparts understand about the Japan subsidiary's role?

Answer: Marketing and sales tend to operate differently from the U.S. Contact with the customer in Japan is so sensitive that sales representatives usually specialize in cultivating particular customer relationships. Marketing takes on the role of liaison with the factory, and acts almost as sales support. This approach frequently upsets headquarters in terms of how much time it takes. They want marketing and sales to push and pull each other as equals. But the Japan subsidiary's system is necessary to keep operations in Japan smooth. The relationship with the customer is so important that the local Japanese rep serves as a sort of buffer between headquarters as well as the overseas factory and the customer. Customers are nurtured by local sales reps, and in a sense protected by them so that they won't have people from headquarters coming at them from all directions.

7. What should Americans understand about Japanese culture to work better with their Japanese counterparts and customers?

Answer: *Tateshakai,* vertical or hierarchical society. Japanese are comfortable with the stability that comes from adherence to status, seniority and rank-ing. As a result, it is important for the U.S. head-quarters to send managers of appropriate rank to meet with their Japanese counterparts and, when necessary, with customers. Not to do so sends the wrong message about the company's level of serious-ness and commitment to the relationship.

Tip: When going on a customer visit in Japan, be sure to clarify with your Japanese team as to your role in the meetings. It is also effective to clarify the relative ranking of the people you'll be meeting with so that you can determine how best to communicate.

1
2
3
4
5
6
7
8

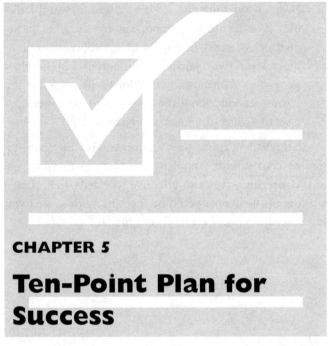

CHAPTER 5

Ten-Point Plan for Success

The more you know about Japanese customs and business practices, the more you can enhance your professional standing with Japanese. Many of our clients seek the "simple" dos and don'ts, and while that approach may never suffice since intercultural situations are so varied, nuanced, and complex, this list is our answer to that question. Even if you read nothing else in this book, it would be a good idea to keep the following list handy, unless, of course, you are able to commit all the points to memory. Ultimately, this list provides you with the main points, or minimum requirements, for doing well in Japan.

Our Top Ten

Business Protocol

1. Bring business cards that are in good condition. Present your card face up and turned so the person you are meeting can read it without having to turn it around. Study the card that you receive and handle it with care.

2. Understand the use of pre-meetings to lay groundwork and build consensus. This will make regular meetings go much more smoothly. Have all materials prepared in Japanese and sent in advance.

3. Meetings are not the place to "hash it out" but to exchange information and confirm consensus. Don't challenge your counterparts, especially in front of customers.

4. Generally refer to Japanese by their last name + *san* (e.g., Tanaka-san), even if they have adopted a Western-sounding first name. In particular avoid using the adopted first name in front of their Japanese peers, as it would sound a bit odd and even unprofessional. In Japanese, the family name comes first and the given name second. If you are working with doctors or professors, refer to them by their last name + *sensei*. Since *san* and *sensei* are terms of honor, you should not append them to your own name.

Communication Style

5. Slow down: Monitor your speaking speed and keep your sentences simple. English is not their native language, nor is English-language proficiency necessar-

ily a measure of competency. Let your counterparts finish their sentences before you speak. Listen more than you speak, and allow for "sidebar" communication and confirmation in Japanese.

6. Leave room in negotiation for a "maybe" instead of forcing a direct "yes" or "no." Indeed, don't expect a direct "no" from Japanese. Don't try to push for an immediate answer or resolution to a business deal (and never at the first meeting). Avoid direct confrontation, which could be met with stonewalling.

7. Don't expect to get direct opinions. Japanese do not find expressing their opinions to be of high value; they tend to want a sense of the group's inclination before saying what they think.

8. Always confirm agreements and next steps.

Relationship Building

9. Relationship is money: Take the time to build good relations. Always assume you'll be in this for the long haul and act accordingly.

10. In general, be alert for ways to make the situation more cooperative and less confrontational. Consider using a trusted third party as a go-between to avoid direct conflict or to mediate a dispute. Your efforts will be appreciated.

Use this Ten-Point Plan as your basic framework. While this may seem like a lot to incorporate, there is no need to stress out about following all the rules at every moment—your genuineness as a person remains an important asset in Japan. Still, it's difficult to overemphasize that Japan is hardly the place to drop in, wing it, and expect to succeed with flying colors.

Beyond the Top Ten

Once you have mastered the top ten, here are a few additional items that will also help ensure your chances for success:

- Bring modest gifts that fit the occasion and rank of the person(s) you are meeting. Don't open gifts unless asked to do so by your Japanese presenter.

- Dress conservatively—good grooming shows seriousness or purpose.

- Follow up. Send notes of thanks—by e-mail is fine. Keep in touch with your partners on a regular basis.

- Reciprocate bowing. Refusing to bow at all in Japan would seem as stand-offish as refusing to shake hands in the U.S. and Europe. While many Japanese will shake hands, they might do it very gently. This is not a sign of weakness.

- Handle items such as gifts or product samples with deliberate care—use two hands whenever possible.

- Pause (count to ten) after asking a question. Use concrete examples, diagrams, illustrations, or flow charts to illustrate your points. Repeat yourself and if necessary, summarize frequently to ensure understanding.

- Note that the use of "yes" or "*hai*" doesn't necessarily mean agreement. It could and often does mean "I'm listening."

- Expect your counterparts to be less direct and use less eye contact. They are only trying to be polite, not disrespectful or secretive.

- Understate rather than exaggerate for effect. Err on the side of modesty and conservatism. Deflect compliments—those directed to you or your colleagues.
- Soften your expressions whenever possible. Instead of "No," or "I disagree," try "It's very difficult," or "My idea is a little different."
- Don't expect Japanese to easily maintain conversation. At least at first, you may have to do most of the work. Stick to everyday topics rather than controversial ones. Help others join in the conversation by inviting comments. Allow for time for translation and confirmation in Japanese.
- Since relationship building is considered a part of doing business, consider very carefully before turning down invitations to dinner or karaoke, even though you may be tired and jetlagged; acceptance is expected. Your spirit of *gambaru* (effort, endurance) won't go unnoticed.

Don't Sweat It If . . .

The following points are offered as an easy way for you to gauge your interactions with Japanese:

. . . nobody asks you questions during or after your presentation. It is considered rude to interrupt speakers during their presentation, because all the information has yet to be presented. Japanese tend to follow deductive reasoning, which means that the conclusion is held until the very end, if offered at all. In addition, many Japanese may also be uncomfortable asking questions in front of others, even at the end of a presentation. They may not want to waste others' time or lose face by asking what could be construed as a "dumb question."

Asking questions could also imply that the speaker wasn't skilled, and they don't want the speaker to lose face by asking a question that might be difficult for him or her to handle.

. . . there is side conversation in Japanese. You might be thinking this is rude or this is poor conduct at a meeting—what are they talking about anyway? Are they talking about me? What's going on? Take a deep breath and let their communication flow. In almost all situations like this the chances are very high that your Japanese counterparts are merely trying to confirm mutual understanding of the last thing you said. Nothing more. Assume that it's part of their flow. If you must ask, try, "Would you like any further clarification?" or "Are we OK?"

. . . people ask rather personal questions. Japanese are often curious about the lives of non-Japanese. Yet, many have never had the opportunity to speak with foreigners. To get to know you, some Japanese may ask questions that you might consider rather blunt and intrusive, for example, about your age, marital status, kids, height, salary, house, religion, and the like. The Japanese are not trying to be intrusive but to learn more about you and find a benchmark of what is typical among foreigners. If you aren't comfortable answering such questions, feel free to deflect them with laughter and a humorous comment. That will usually be the end of it. By the way, for some Japanese, such questions may represent the extent of their ability in English, the only way they know to keep the conversation moving.

. . . your Japanese counterparts get rather drunk after hours. This is a natural by-product of after-hours socialization and is a sign that everyone is having a good time. Being slightly inebriated promotes relaxation, and, as some Japanese will tell you, better English. You can be the judge of that! The silliness that comes with feeling tipsy revs up the humor, the group banter, and the courage to try a few rounds of karaoke. Don't be surprised if the next day your Japanese colleagues are back to being stone-faced and no one talks about the previous evening; no one, then, has to cope with the embarrassment of what may have happened during the night.

. . . your Japanese counterparts plan your schedule, including every free minute on the weekend. Hosting guests in Japan includes "taking care of someone from start to finish." Japanese will be concerned about your "down time" and may want to plan events so that you are not left to fend for yourself. They want you to enjoy the full range of activities available in their country. On the second and third nights of your stay, when jetlag seems stronger than ever, try not to decline an invitation since this very well could be to a dinner that has been carefully planned long before you arrived.

. . . you hear "We will do our best" or "I'll do my best." In the U.S., this might sound slightly negative, depending on the situation. Japanese who use this English phrase, however, mean to express total commitment, as in the Japanese expression "*Gambarimasu.*"

. . . you don't get to see the head person right away. Japan's hierarchical society restricts access to the upper echelons of an organization. Japanese middle managers will want to size you up before introducing you to their top officers. Be patient and remain scrupulously professional and affable with everyone you meet. Japan is a group-oriented society and, in the end, no one person—not even a top officer—will single-handedly decide to buy your product or agree to your proposal.

. . . even when you use some Japanese, the listener responds to you in English. It's not meant to be a criticism of your limited Japanese or non-native pronunciation. Rather, many Japanese, who have learned English since high school or earlier, may wish to seize an opportunity to use some of what they have learned. Moreover, in the presence of their compatriots, many Japanese will want to be seen using English as opposed to rudimentary Japanese.

. . . you don't get any feedback. In Japan, no news truly may be good news. Suffice it to say that if there is no constructive criticism or any comment whatsoever, you're probably right on target. This can be quite frustrating for Westerners who are accustomed to more frequent feedback.

It's Time to Worry If . . .

. . . you hear the sound of air being sucked through teeth. This is a classic indicator that the issue under discussion is problematic. Rather than rushing to modify or add to what you have said, try first to determine what is causing your counterparts to respond in such a way.

. . . you hear such responses as "That's difficult" or "It's under investigation." These responses indicate a negative reply, like "Thanks, but no thanks." To learn the underlying reasons, it's best at this point to do more listening than speaking.

. . . you are pushed to work faster or complete something sooner. This very likely means that an important customer's needs are not being met. Get on your horse. Meeting customers' needs to the nth degree is sacrosanct in Japan.

. . . you've arrived in Japan to negotiate a deal and nobody's at work. Whoops! This could be a problem, unless you intend to do some sightseeing. Three holiday periods—New Year's (*Oshogatsu*), Golden Week, and *Obon*—lasting for about one week each, are times when little business gets done. *Oshogatsu*, covering the end of December into early January, is perhaps Japan's biggest holiday season. Golden Week includes three national holidays, beginning with Green Day on April 29, Constitution Day on May 3, and Childrens' Day on the first Saturday in May. *Obon*, occurring on the 13 to 15 of July or August (depending on the region), is a Buddhist holiday when many people return to their hometowns to pay respect to their ancestors. Not only is business at a standstill during these periods, but so many people are traveling that it can be difficult getting tickets to travel in or outside of Japan. For a full list of Japanese holidays, please see page 255.

Questions You Might Not Be Expecting

As mentioned earlier in this section, Japanese, whether out of curiosity or simply a lack of vocabulary, often ask rather personal questions of their foreign counterparts. Perhaps the best way to respond might be through laughter, humor, and asking the questioner to guess at the answer. For example, if someone asks how old you are—assuming you don't want to answer—simply ask that person to guess your age. At that point, the issue becomes moot rather quickly. Following is a list of such questions, some of which you may not mind answering.

- How old are you?
- What are your hobbies? What do you do in your free time?
- Do you play golf? What is your handicap?
- Do you like Japanese food? Can you eat sushi? Can you use chopsticks? What Japanese foods can't you eat?
- Where is your family? How is your family? Are they well?
- Do you have any children? How many children do you have? Why don't you have any children?
- Is your spouse OK? (Often asked of women traveling alone.)
- How much does your company pay you? How much does your house cost?
- When did you graduate from college? What was your major?
- What's your blood type? This question reflects the widely held belief in Japan that blood types correlate with certain personality types, similar to Zodiac signs (e.g., those with type A blood are astute businesspeople.) You can really have fun with this conversation, providing you know your blood type.

The bottom line: Assume the best. Assume that the miscommunication or unfamiliar behavior might be due to cultural differences. Try to keep your defensiveness in check. And at all times maintain a sense of humor.

CHAPTER 6

Trends in a Global Japan

The Japanese Marketplace and Society

Although change is afoot in Japan, it might appear glacial by Western standards. Understanding what is changing and what is not—and the connection between them—is crucial to business success in Japan.

About Consumer Behavior and Products

Here is Japan at the cutting edge: un-peopled robotic manufacturing lines; just-in-time inventory and production techniques; advanced public transportation that truly is convenient; heated carpeting (shoes are not worn in their homes); inexpensive next-day delivery of just about anything; 7-Elevens that offer everything from a hot, fresh meal to online banking services; wireless telephone proliferation that has surpassed line-based phone lines; bullet trains that go about as fast as a speeding bullet; toilets that give you an extra rinse and blow dry; rice cookers that talk while they fix rice twelve different ways; microwave convection ovens; the most sophisticated computer games in the world; singing washing machines; mobile phones that do everything from connect you to the Internet and live video chats to downloading your favorite TV programs; and on and on.

A quick look around the various Japanese department stores and electronics-goods shops confirms Japan as a global leader in manufacturing and marketing consumer products.

Yet, in spite of their advanced digital technologies, many Japanese still favor some analog approaches—such as hanging their laundry outside to dry. On a sunny day, this gives Japanese apartment buildings an almost surreal, third world appearance. Such apparent technological-social contradictions are widely seen in Japan today.

Japanese Rigor about Quality

Japan is still the standard bearer when it comes to manufacturing quality. Zero tolerance for defects and Deming's methods, while not invented in Japan, were famously put into practice there.

Japanese consumers expect a product to be right the first time. And they don't have the space to store lots of spares. Brand becomes more important when you must trust that the thing you buy is what you'll be stuck with; in Japan, there is almost never a money-back or satisfaction guarantee. The attitude, "If I don't like it, I can just take it back," which is standard in the U.S. and other countries, is not assumed in Japan. In fact, most Japanese would be embarrassed to take something back; it would reflect poor judgment on the part of the buyer. It would also upset the prevailing harmony by explicitly violating the original trust with the maker/seller about glitch-free products.

What Do Japanese Consumers Really Want?

The chart below summarizes observations about buying and selling patterns in Japan, as compared with the U.S. Do your products or services measure up?

Japan	U.S.
Does it meet spec? (Form)	Does it do the job? (Function)
Is it scratch-free? Look perfect? Goods with perceived imperfections won't sell.	Can I live with it? Did I get a discount? Volume discount?
If broken: Find root cause, ensure customer of correction.	If broken: Take it back and get another one.
If I don't have one, will I fall behind?	If I get one, will it help me get ahead?
Is it cute? User friendly? Trendy?	Is it cool? Fast? Powerful? Fun?
Is it the latest model? Is it top end? Brand name?	Is it on sale? Do I have a coupon? Better shop around.
Is it the best-selling model?	Is it rated highly in Consumer Reports?
Options are standard, should be loaded with basic features.	Save money without those pricey options, minimize unnecessary features.
"After service" is free, quality is expected. "Take it back" isn't an option.	Pay for service (get what you pay for), pay more for quality.
The customer is god.	Drive the customer toward better solutions.

Notes on Manufacturing: Form Over Function?

The typical, cost-effective Western approach to manufacturing is to make lots of product, expecting a small quota of defects but allowing frequent upgrades (necessary in a rapidly changing field). In Japan, that won't work. Let's say that your company sells a semiconductor chip to an OEM manufacturer in Japan. New technologies and market forces cause you to switch that chip with another that has value-added features and higher processing speed. Yet when you proudly offer the new product to your Japanese customer, even at the same price as the old one, it is soundly rejected.

Buying power of young women and housewives: Will it help my children get ahead? Does everyone else have one?	Buying power of baby-boomers: Will it improve my quality of life? Is it a good investment?
Newer must be better.	Buying used items is smart, economical.
Many foreign-made products are lower in quality.	Buy anything that works and is cost effective.
Promotion, free gifts, impeccable presentation.	Shelf space, catchy displays.
Established corporate image, reputation, and brand name.	Can earn a reputation, clever ideas sell, new companies have fresh ideas.
Specialty shops, vending machines, convenience stores, direct mail, or Internet order: 1–2 day delivery.	Everything is at the superstore 24/7; orders over the phone and Internet: 7–10 day delivery. Express delivery costs extra.
Shop every day (fresh is critical—limited storage space).	Shop once a week (convenience is critical—lots of storage space).
Gadgets.	Tools.
Image.	Value.

They want to know, "Where is the chip we ordered?" That's the one that their manufacturer is expecting, that has been given all the inspections and quality and stress testing, and that will be included in their new product launch. The new chip, however good it is, will cause their assembly lines to halt (while they do the required inspections and testing) and force a delay in launch. In fact, from a Japanese perspective, if the new semiconductor is even cosmetically different from the old product specifications, it may not be perceived as compatible with the equipment for which it was originally intended. For example, the manufacturer's robotic vision or other quality sensors might not recognize it, and it will then be deemed defective. Product improvement, especially fast-track product migration and upgrading, may seem a matter of common sense in the U.S., but in Japan change is not taken simply as a matter of course; it must be scrutinized in depth from every angle. Quality must be assured at all cost.

Sample Scenario: Bulb Burnout

The quality level of a particular U.S. company's light bulbs—many failed on first use—was unacceptable for the Japanese market. Even so, the company's American marketing manager pushed to sell the bulbs for industrial use in packs of a hundred. That suggestion struck his Japanese joint-venture colleagues as ridiculous—no one buys so many bulbs at once. The marketing manager felt that the Japanese expectations of quality and sales were unrealistic and unnecessarily expensive. "You can't expect them all to work," he maintained. "And by purchasing them in bulk, the customer will pay less, and still have plenty of good ones." His Japanese counterparts couldn't imagine that their U.S. partner had so little common sense. Didn't he know anything about Japan before coming here to do business? As it turns out, this particular joint venture failed.

A Changing Japan: Into the Information Age

Let's explore the major trends that affect how business is conducted in Japan. What can we expect as Japan transitions from *keiretsu* to *net-batsu* to wireless and beyond, and to entering into new global partnerships? And what of the IPO craze, deregulation, Japan's slow rise out of its economic doldrums, the critical areas where Japan appears light years ahead of—or in some cases behind—the rest of the world?

Japan has been the second largest economy in the world for decades, and yet the stagnation in the economy has been rampant since the early 1990s. Evidence of Japan's trailing position can be found in the employment figures: in the year 2000, unemployment in Japan reached its highest point in fifty years (4.9 percent), surpassing that of the U.S. for the first time since World War II. The one ray of hope came in the form of the Internet boom of the late '90s and early '00s. In spite of the dot-com bust of 2000, the growth of the Internet caused a wave of entrepreneurism such as Japan had not seen since the building boom after World War II. Japan might actually be warming to the notion of extensive change to avoid falling further behind in the globally networked economy. Indeed, as of 2007 it appears that the Japanese economy is finally back on track. Growth in 2006 outpaced the U.S. and most European countries.

Evidence of Change

Change appears to be coming, though at an uneven pace. Big bank mergers such as Mizuho Holdings and Sumitomo Mitsui would have been unheard of just a few years ago, especially between former rivals. Historically resistant to foreign investment, Japan took in a record ¥12 trillion (US$100 billion) in FDI stock in 2005, at least four times the figure for 1998, and the numbers continue to rise. For the first time ever, Japanese banks are now being sold to foreign entities. In the early '00s, value, rather than image alone, began to influence buying decisions. The former craze for Gucci and Yves Saint-Laurent for a time was largely replaced by more cost-effective shopping at trendy concept retailers such as the revolutionary low-priced Uniqlo (pronounced "uni-clo") casual clothing chain, Muji (no-name brands) or the more mainstream but also value-conscious Gap and Brooks Brothers. Even the brand-name department stores, which had in the past taken great pride in offering only full-priced items, began offering storewide bargain sales. And some of the most posh, centrally located hotels offered half-price discount coupons to lure these more cost-conscious business travelers. Now the tide has turned once again: the posh stores are back in full force, but they are selling right next door to the equally inviting value stores.

What is hastening the pace of change now? The Japanese economy has been under pressure for years to deregulate. Historically and today, foreign pressure, or *gaiatsu*, has certainly played a role in initiating such advances. For example, in the 1990s U.S.-based Motorola used political means to pressure the Japanese government into deregulating the mobile-phone market. While the Japanese mobile-phone-industry proponents complained loudly about this use of force, they moved in with lightning speed to capitalize on the opportunities that opened up in the newly deregulated phone market. Observers of change also point to the dawn of the information age and the role of the Internet as a major change agent. While investment in information technology has leveled off in recent years, in 2000, 25 percent of Japan's capital outlays went for high-tech products, up from 15 percent in 1998. Even the big companies are getting wired. Toshiba and Fujitsu are retooling to focus their efforts on IT. NEC claims that as much as 25 percent of its business is being conducted online. Sony has partnered with the former Sakura Bank, now part of Sumitomo Mitsui, in setting up its own online bank. In 2007, Japan is set to overtake the U.S. as the biggest consumer of online goods.

Japan's Internet population is growing by leaps and bounds. Indeed, according to JETRO 2005 figures, 66 percent of Japan's total population was online via PC, and 70 percent via mobile phone or PDA. Broadband penetration had already reached the 23 million mark (18 percent of the population). Wireless access is all the rage, with NTT's DoCoMo taking the lead with its iMode services. By the end of 2000, iMode boasted 10 million customers, and some 50 million worldwide in 2005. Via iMode, it is possible to do such things as read and send e-mail, do your online banking, check the weather and train schedules, and access cartoons to clip and send to your buddies, download the latest best-selling book, even view your favorite TV shows and movies. You can use your mobile phone to have a two-way video conference from wherever you happen to be.

For the first time ever, big companies like Sony are selling directly to the end user online. This included some 40 percent of PlayStation 2 sales. Cutting out the middleman is a very new concept in Japan, but those who resist will probably be left in the dust. Being able to move quickly and cut costs is becoming a survival must, even for the global corporations.

There are compelling examples of young entrepreneurs breaking all the rules in the new era. The most famous story would have to be about Masayoshi Son of SoftBank who started out on his own buying software houses and technology publishers. In the Internet boom of the late '90s, his company rose to prominence as a leader in all areas of Internet technology, most notably in startup incubation and venture capital. Son saw his little company rise to become one of the most influential in Japan. By 2007, SoftBank had become one of the key players in the mobile-phone business in Japan with an innovative flat-fee type of plan. Son is still the one of the richest men in Asia, and his company continues to be one of the most influential.

Japan's tradition-bound culture has served the country well for hundreds of years. From the ashes of WWII, Japan rose to world dominance in almost every industrial arena. When it comes to manufacturing, Japan is still tops in the world and remains the benchmark for quality worldwide. But the Japanese formula, with its finicky attention to detail and zero defects, isn't an unqualified strength in the rapidly advancing knowledge-based economy. Perhaps Japan needs to recover its historical tendency to borrow the best from the rest of the world, as usual in a way that is uniquely Japanese. We believe it will.

Values Shift: What the Experts Say

Are the underlying Japanese values changing as a result of the changes in society and business? In January of 2000, a government-commissioned advisory panel suggested that individuals in group-oriented Japan be empowered and that students spend more time being creative. Could there be change afoot in the herd mentality?

David Cook, international business consultant who

has handled U.S.-Japan business dealings in several industrial sectors, including telecommunications and e-commerce, over the past twenty-plus years had this to say:

> In Japan, conformity to the group is a deeply rooted value, starting from an early age. Japanese society still regards displays of individual excellence with suspicion, as reflected in the oft-cited adage: "The nail that sticks up gets hammered down." The ultimate criticism for Japanese is "Others will laugh at you" rather than, as in many Western countries, "You are not good enough." Not surprisingly, therefore, Japanese corporations continue to rely on time-consuming, consensus-based decision-making processes. This does not bode well in an era where lightning speed is required just to stay afloat, never mind getting ahead.

What Cook is saying is that fundamentally, the criteria for success in the Japanese market are shifting. For the past sixty years, the path to success in Japan was simple and well understood by all pursuing it. A care-free childhood was exchanged for study, with the prospect of gaining admission to a prestigious university, which guaranteed employment by elite companies. Boundless effort, commitment, and loyalty were poured into the company, and with any luck one stayed inside of the hierarchical triangle and retired in the company of a select cadre of paternal leaders. The criteria for advancement lay in the depth of one's social skills, and the ability to shepherd consensus in the "family." Creative initiatives and individual promotion go against you in this system, and until recently compensation has been largely blind to merit. In contrast, the information economy, with few barriers to entry in many sectors, is driven primarily on creative breakthroughs, the vision of individuals, and highly qualified team efforts that are compensated proportionately to success.

What Japanese Officials Say

So how has Japan really responded to the needs of the new economy? In the early '00s even well-established Japanese government officials were talking up their optimism about the current transition. In a keynote address to the Japan Society in 2001, Japan's then–Ambassador to the U.S., the Honorable Shunji Yanai, outlined the following major projected transitions:

Changes in education: An English-language initiative is underway, and education is moving away from absolute conformity and encouraging entrepreneurship.

Deregulation: We are now seeing more of the positive effects of deregulation and corporate restructuring in terms of more streamlined and competitive companies.

Lifetime employment: This is no longer a given, even in the name-brand corporations. Job-hopping is slowly becoming less stigmatized.

Foreign investment in Japan: The amount quadrupled from 1998 to 1999, and is expected to rise further. In 2003 Prime Minister Koizumi reiterated the goal of doubling foreign investment by 2010.

Engaging in a more global role: Japan has plans to increase foreign aid, bolster its Self-Defense forces, and possibly take on a less passive global role.

Of the above initiatives, we have seen all of these come to fruition in some form or other by the late 2000s. It remains to be seen that they result in major shifts in the values and underpinnings of Japanese society.

Values Shift: Changed, but How Deeply?

So that still leaves us with the question, how deep are the changes in Japan? Are they really becoming more Westernized? Our answer is "No"—Japan is changing and modernizing, but becoming, if anything, more Japanese. In a 2000 interview, Masayuki Kohama, a Japanese entrepreneur, author, and international business consultant, stated, "Japanese need to take on two modes: a Japanese mode and a global mode. The entire society needs to change to rise to the global challenge." His prediction/urging has in some ways come true in that Japan has woken up and smelled the Starbucks (680 Starbucks stores in Japan as of 2006) and other global companies—and their business methods—that are suddenly thrusting themselves upon her shores. But does having more shopping options and non-Japanese business partnerships constitute deep change?

Currently, Japan is witnessing a swing in the Japanese service industry toward information services and products. The experience has given many an ambitious entrepreneur a vision of possibilities and quick fortunes. This change of mindset by a capable, fresh generation of businesspeople is a potentially fatal fissure in the stone-cast institutions of Japan, Inc. The seniority-based structure of business institutions is meeting a healthy challenge from a meritocracy model. Japanese are struggling with the conflicting ideals of consensus and creativity. Also, as in any market, the introduction of state-of-the-art IT tools, particularly the Internet, Intranets, Extranets, and the like, is structurally morphing Japanese business practices. Many recent editorials lament or exalt the death of the middleman. This is especially consequential in Japan, where a large portion of the service sector has traditionally acted as the middleman.

Takafumi Horie: "The Nail That Sticks Up"

One highly visible example of a businessperson taking on the system came in the form of Takafumi Horie, better known as "Horiemon." Horie is a Japanese entrepreneur extraordinaire who founded Livedoor, a Web site design operation that grew into a highly successful Internet portal involved in a wide range of businesses. He rose to prominence very quickly thanks to his entrepreneurial acumen and his unconventional methods—everything from his practice of corporate expansion through acquisitions to his informal attire. He rarely wore a necktie and suit, preferring T-shirts and brightly-colored sweaters. The media had a field day—on the one hand taking him to task over his challenges to the status quo, while on the other capitalizing on the star appeal of his nonconformist business attitude and lavish lifestyle.

In 2005, Horie bought a large number of shares in Fuji Television and attempted a widely publicized hostile takeover—the battle for Fuji TV was the most watched TV show at the time. Soon after, Japan introduced M&A laws to prevent this type of incident from reoccurring.

In 2006, Horie was arrested on accusations of securities fraud. He severed all connections with his former company. His trial began in the fall of 2006. Many felt that Horie's treatment was a political move by defenders of the status quo. The old guard wanted to "hammer down the nail that sticks up," to punish Horie for daring to take them on, and to discredit him and the business practices he had come to represent, practices they consider distasteful and "un-Japanese." In March of 2007, Horie was sentenced to a jail term of two years and six months.

The Horie incident does not portend any quick

changes as the information economy forces a clash between the more U.S.-like model and the traditional model of Japan, Inc. with its monolithic institutions created by the *zaibatsu* and their political connections. When the Internet boom went bust in 2001, the old guard had plenty of "I told you sos" to fire off. And throughout, well-established "old economy" foreign companies such as IBM, Proctor and Gamble, Johnson & Johnson, Boeing, and Intel managed to survive and thrive. And former dot-com SoftBank has reinvented itself and reemerged as one of the most successful high-tech companies in Japan. Ultimately, who will win? To the extent that we understand information economics, the Western model might seem to be better suited for the fast paced new economy. On the other hand, if the Japanese find a "bamboo solution" (bend it, but don't break it), they may spontaneously innovate a new advancement in the information economy and boom right past an unsuspecting world.

While it remains to be seen if they will boom right past, there may yet be a place in Japan's future for pioneers like Horie in a new Japanese economy. Japan is without a doubt the most technologically advanced country in a fast-growing Asia, and are well positioned in their unique role as one of the strongest, most influential players in both the East and West.

Japan's Global Role

Why Japan Is Still an Attractive Place to Do Business

Why Japan? Why Now?

It is a well-known fact that Japan has a solid, modernized system, well-established infrastructure, and world class, top-ranking industries. Unlike emerging economies and BRIC countries, there are important similarities between Japan and the U.S. and European businesses when it comes to business sense, capitalism, and efficiency. The flow of capital and business relationships between U.S. -Japan-Europe has been established over a period of decades. The Western countries still have a lot to learn from Japanese sense of quality and service sense, so the game is far from over. (M. Kohama, 2007)

The Boomers Are Coming

There is one more reason to pay close attention to Japan right now: In the next two to three years (2007–10), the largest population group of post–WWII baby boomers are set to retire at age sixty. The Baby Boomers are coming, and thanks to the post–WWII pension system, they have disposable incomes to burn. All together, they will be paid more than ¥15 trillion (US$120 billion) in severance pay per year, amounting to a total of ¥50 trillion (US$480 billion), with personal assets of approximately ¥130 trillion (US$1.2 trillion)—a sum that is equal to the 2006 GDP of India and Brazil combined. No one is sure exactly what this wave of retirement will mean for Japan. Will these conscientious seniors hold tight and stash away their hard-earned yen carefully for the long term, or will they release decades of pent-up demand? The members of this population group are generally well educated, have a variety of hobbies, are interested in ongoing educational and travel opportunities and "are expected to become a pillar of domestic consumption in Japan" (JETRO 2006). Does your company have a strategy to capture any part of this very attractive emerging market?

China and Japan

Perhaps you remain unconvinced by the points above, and are thinking of the allure of China, perhaps in hopes that it's much easier to do business there. No one will deny that China can potentially offer huge opportunities for anyone who can manage to finesse the system there. China has risen to number six among the world's biggest economies. Already the Chinese economy is in the number two spot when looked at in terms of the country's purchasing-power parity (*Pocket Economist World in Figures*, 2007), and China will eventually surpass Japan as an economic power by sheer mass.

Many large global companies and smaller SME's have sunk large chucks of their fortune into China, betting on the vitality of this booming nation. So should you bypass Japan and head full speed ahead to do business in China? Elaine Kurtenbach of the Associated Press had this to say in May of 2007:

> Across China, foreign businesses are facing new challenges as authorities raise taxes and tighten controls on mergers and acquisitions and real estate dealings. Regulations have added new hurdles to doing business in a country where the law is most often a tool used to protect the powerful.
>
> "Doing business in China is not for the meek," says Laurence Brahm, a former consultant and author of numerous books on the subject.
>
> Some failures have involved big name companies. Avon has seen its dreams for hefty profits

diminished by legal changes [for foreign companies in China]. Carlyle, a powerful private investment fund, saw its plans to take over heavy-equipment maker Xugong Group Construction Machinery Co. disrupted by nationalist opposition.

Let's look at China from a different angle:

On the Human Development index, China is not in the top sixty, while Japan is no. 11. China's GDP per head is $1,470. Japan's is $36,170, and the United States' is $39,430.

China is still a risky place to do business. One way to possibly reduce some of that risk is by going through an intermediary. Some kind of connection, no matter how remote, can help to ensure a smoother relationship, and can spread the business risk. One approach might be to go through Japan and your Japanese associates to get to China. That's right. While there may be political tensions between the two countries, the trade between them—which, by the way, has been going on for centuries—has absolutely exploded in the 21st century. China and Japan seem to both have a "mutual admiration society" and love-hate relationship all at the same time.

> **From the 2007 Japan External Trade Organization (JETRO) Report, "Ten Advantages to Investing in Japan"**
>
> - World's second-largest market.
> - Sophisticated consumers with high purchasing power.
> - World-class companies and SMEs (small- to medium-sized enterprises) with unique technologies.
> - Loyalty and commitment to long-term partnerships.
> - World's center for technological innovation and product development.
> - Access to new Asian markets.
> - Favorable business climate.
> - Rapidly growing broadband society.
> - Expanding environmental market.
> - Booming business in silver care and retirees.

There are many Japanese companies and agents who can help you get connected, and give you guidance in China. Japan has been dancing with China for thousands of years, as the countries are right next door to each other. So don't cross Japan off your Asian strategy; if you can make it there, you'll make it anywhere—Japan and China go *way* back.

As East Asia grows, economies are becoming more service-oriented. Common tastes are developing and lifestyles are converging, in particular in urban areas. Many consumer products that gain popularity in Japan, including movies, *anime*, game software, clothing, and cosmetics, go on to become popular in East Asia in general. Success in Japan is a litmus test for success in East Asia. (JETRO 2007)

The New Japan

What's the Same, What's Changed, What's Sustainable

While it may seem that Japan has changed drastically in recent years, it might not be at the deepest levels. We've come to this conclusion based on our observations, research and ongoing work, interactions, and life-long relationships. When it comes to culture, the old adage holds true: "The more things change, the more they stay the same." Especially in the face of adversity and catastrophe, it is human nature to go to one's most comfortable and familiar roots and exhibit behaviors that are consistent with that home culture. This is true even for people who claim to be at the edges of the bell curve of what is "typical" to their culture. Of course Japan is changing and modern-

Things Japan Has Retained in the Last Few Decades	Ways Japan Has Changed in the 21st Century
Hard working, long hours, two-hour commute still the norm, telecommuting rare, flex time not widely practiced.	Younger workers less inclined to give all private time to company. More foreign workers to fill growing labor shortages.
Homogeneous, 99% ethnically Japanese, tendency to adjust to fit in (*awase*), strong *uchi/soto* (in-group/out-group) feelings about belonging.	Greater foreign presence: South Americans, SE Asians, and Indians who work hard but may have as much difficulty adjusting to Japan as Westerners.
Collectivism, desire to be "upstanding" (and within societal norms) rather than "outstanding."	Some Japanese have a specific personal style. Regulations have changed to better support entrepreneurs.
Quality-focused, zero defects. Emphasis on brand names, luxury goods; desire for "genuine" brands/items.	Boom in both low- and high-end shopping: imports from China and no-brand shopping alongside major luxury-goods stores.
Tateshakai (vertical society): seniority still in place, unofficially. Desire to establish/understand each person's role.	Meritocracy has become widespread, younger people in managerial roles, more mid-career hires and temporary workers.
The need to build consensus: *nemawashi* (ground work), *ringi* (approval rounds).	Desire to speed up the decision-making process; use of electronic communication.
Having lifetime employment is still "the Japanese Dream."	Restructuring/downsizing a reality, more mid-career hiring, use of head-hunters, flexibility in the job market, temps.
Emphasis on education, cram schools, high literacy rate.	Young people dropping out of the system (*hikikomori*, NEETs, and *furita*); concern about education level of public schools.
Importance of business entertainment.	Not as mandatory: people value their "private time" more.

izing, but it's at Japan's own pace and according to what works for Japan, as illustrated in the chart here.

The biggest danger is to assume that the more Japan changes, the more they become "just like us."

Japan's Influences Around the World

- Automotive Industry: Since WWII Japan has been tenaciously building toward world-market

Consumers' attention to detail: picking the right product, restaurant atmosphere, etc.	Use of Internet to get the most current information and bargains (*Rakuten* e-shopping mall, etc.).
Attention to form or *kata*: business card exchange, new hires in "uniform" black suits.	New kinds of *kata*: mobile phone etiquette ("manner mode"), "cool biz" fashion.
"Japan is a resource-poor, small island nation" mentality.	Japan is very strong in the Internet economy; rising nationalism.
Smoking still at almost 60-plus percent among men.	More special areas for smoking (i.e., specific smoking hours at restaurants, coffee shops).
Spoken English still a struggle. Some overseas executives reluctant to use local language.	Studying at earlier ages, more "professional" English-language schools and ESL programs, including intercultural training.
Most women assume role of homemaker. Child care outside family not widely available, not universally accepted.	Women delaying marriage; more female entrepreneurs, start-up companies run by women. Handful of male homemakers.
Companies reluctant to provide forecasts, budget estimates. Extensive contingency planning.	Companies want to be streamlined, responsive to change, but without deviating from Japanese business standards.
Lots of drinking, smoking.	More consciousness about health, organic goods; less tolerance for public drunkenness.

dominance in the automotive industry. Finally, in 2007, for the first time ever, Japanese automaker Toyota surpassed GM in terms of car sales. While other automakers might be struggling to maintain a foothold in their own markets, Toyota, with its top-down quality obsession, has been steadily and persistently raising the quality bar and selling its always-reliable, technologically advanced cars even in the most remote corners of the planet.

- Consumer Gadgetry: Even if they were not all invented in Japan, the Japanese have taken many of these items to their fullest potential: GameBoy and PlayStation video/computer games, DVD, HDTV, MP3, and now wireless Internet connection and video conferencing via cell phones. In spite of tough global competition, Japan shows no signs of relinquishing its lead in this area. We've come a very long way from the cheap "Made in Japan" image of several decades ago.

- Production Standards: When it comes to advanced manufacturing processes and superior quality of goods produced, Japan still rules. With the goal of zero defects and severe stress testing, Japanese production standards are undoubtedly the most stringent anywhere and serve as the benchmark for producers of goods worldwide. And if your product can possibly be made smaller, lighter, cheaper, or better, you can bet that Japanese engineers are hard at work on it already.

- Energy Efficiency: Japan puts many other countries, especially the U.S., to shame when it comes to energy efficiency, far outpacing them in the ongoing development of sustainable manufacturing processes, environmentally clean processes, and even in home appliances.

- Japanese Cuisine: Sushi is already a household word in most developed countries and the rich variety of Japanese noodles is not far behind. Going out for these once-exotic dishes no longer raises eyebrows in Minneapolis, London, or Rio de Janeiro. Additionally, the links between the Japanese diet and the amazing life expectancy of Japanese citizens have hardly been ignored by the international community: Japanese staples such as soybeans, tofu, green tea, ginger, and soymilk have also become much more common in many countries. Now the Japanese government is considering instituting a certification process for Japanese restaurants to ensure that even food served abroad meets basic standards to be called "Japanese."

- Spirituality: Japanese spirituality, anchored in Buddhism and Shintoism, will continue to become better known around the world, with increasing interest in meditation, the notion of karma, and the sanctity of nature. Simpler, Asian-influenced interior design, table-top fountains, rock gardens, aromatherapy, and shiatsu massage call to mind the serenity of Zen.

- Designers: From fashion to landscaping, Japanese designers are becoming more recognized internationally. In the future, the design world will become infiltrated with Japanese players, some of whom are already enjoying worldwide fame.

- Animation: Japanese *anime* has become state of the art, as with any of the Miyazaki films, or for example, *Pokemon* and *Yu-Gi-Oh!* and a host of other characters and movies. *Anime* comes to us in the highest-tech computer games on the planet. It has clearly influenced the art of animation around the world. We heard of one young *anime* fan in the U.S. selecting a Japanese emersion middle school in order to better understand the subtleties of her passion.

- Export of Pop Culture: For years, Japanese pop culture has flourished all over Asia via music, movies, fashion, and gadgetry. Recently Japan has become a testing ground for new fashion and apparel concepts and products. Often, fashion retailers roll out their new goods in Tokyo, making Japan's capital the hottest new pilot market for anything deemed "cool." Japan's pop culture debut outside of Asia is only beginning.

Predictions and Trends

Hierarchies Turned Sideways

The shock waves of the information age and the clash of the new economy with the old economy will bring more restructuring. Japanese will be increasingly open to new and foreign models for change and imported change-management expertise. Strategic alliances, joint ventures, and partnering opportunities, already widespread, will increase, exposing Japan to the effects of global diversity. The desultory economy of the last decade has been a boon to outplacement and recruiting firms. This phenomenon will only increase as the economy improves while the working population falls. The workforce is gradually becoming more mobile, with more job-hopping, mid-career hiring, and opportunities for new companies to hire experienced talent along with the new college grads. There will also be a greater willingness to take risks. The once "vertical society" (*tateshakai*) will need to invent new ways to interact as conventions such as age and length of time at one company or name of one's university are less and less the barometers of status. We do not predict that the hierarchy will be flattened—it will just take on new, always Japanese, forms.

Global Partnering, Foreign CEOs

There is a current openness to building partnerships where exclusivity had once been the rule. The opportunity to create business partnerships in Japan has never been better. Business-to-business innovations abound, as Japanese companies attempt to take full advantage of their advanced technology. Some fairly recent examples include Sony and Toshiba partnering with IBM to make the next generation of semiconductors, and Rolls Royce partnering with the National Institute for Materials Science to make new heat-resistant alloys. The partnerships will increasingly be with Asia-based companies in emerging markets. Another example of openness will come in the form of allowing more non-Japanese to head up major Japanese corporations. Former head of Nissan, Carlos Ghosen, and Sir Howard Stringer of Sony already have stood out as capable non-local talent who could get the job done.

> One of the advantages of doing business in Japan is that while it takes quite a bit of time to enter into

a contract, once you do, those relationships are for the long term. Because there is little switching between vendors, unlike in the West, a company can look forward to stable and long-lasting revenue from its Japanese partners. (Security middleware provider, JETRO 2007)

Declining Population and Workforce Changes

In response to the declining population and workforce entrants, the question remains "Which route will Japan take?" Will Japan create new enticements for women to have more kids while still working, such as attractive day-care options, flexible work hours, or options to work from home? Will Japan do more to re-employ the still-energetic retired seniors who have the knowledge, skills, and experience that still needs to be passed on? Or will Japan need to open its shores to a limited immigrant population, eager to work hard and learn from the most advanced companies in the world? We've seen examples of all three of these starting to happen in Japan. For example, we interviewed a contract engineer from India who had been recruited to work in IT in Japan. For him, working in Japan presented an opportunity to gain experience fast: thanks to the long working hours, India considers job experience in Japan to be double the same time period in India. Other industries, such as heavy manufacturing, which are having a hard time attracting young Japanese workers for blue-collar jobs, are increasingly turning to foreign help in spite of the fact that the workers won't be staying more than a few years.

Innovative Products for an Aging Population

In 2005, Japan already had the highest population aged

sixty and over (26.3 percent—*Economist Pocket World in Figures*, p. 20) and the highest median age. The proportion of the elderly, sixty-five years and above, in the total population could be as high as one-third in fifty years. The number of households with persons over sixty-five has more than doubled in the last twenty-five years. These seniors will need new task-enabling products. According to JETRO, "The growth of senior consumers is generating new needs in the medical, health, and nursing care fields. The market scale of these fields is expected to increase to ¥75 trillion by 2010." Specially designed computers, with voice recognition, and websites for seniors will be in greater demand. Modes of transportation will increasingly accommodate seniors. Convenience stores are increasingly stocking up on products that appeal to the over-sixty-five set, as the older generation begins to show willingness to choose convenience over familiarity. Innovative companies have already come out with robotic nurses who can do simple tasks for the elderly. Home security systems with cameras and sensor-triggered lighting are already taking off.

Other Innovative Products, Services, and Scientific Breakthroughs

In 2006 Japan ranked third in terms of GDP spending on Research and Development, above the U.S., Germany, and France, and was number three in the world in terms of growth of patent applications in 2005. Japan also ranked highest in terms of innovation on the Summary Innovation Index in 2005. We can expect Japan to bring us robots to help the whole family, medicines to alleviate or cure major diseases such as Alzheimer's and even cancer, environmentally friendly products to increase recycling and reduce pollution, entertainment electronics that take HDTV to the next level, whatever that might be (Smell? Taste?). Japan leads the way in terms of convenience-store innovation. From delivery to packaging to added services such as overnight delivery and banking, 7-Eleven for example has become such a successful market driver that it now works directly with manufacturers to create products and packaging specifically for its clientele. In the future, they may include pharmacy and other services for seniors as well.

> Japanese consumers are early adopters and move fast to stay on the cutting edge of the latest technologies. Most companies in Japan listen carefully to consumer demands when developing new products, as many products in common use around the world have originated in Japan. Japan thus makes an ideal test market for new products and services. (JETRO 2007)

Changes in Medical Care

In spite of being perhaps the world's preeminent supplier of cutting edge medical devices, Japan is only just beginning to take advantage of its own technology at home. Among the many trends in this area are:

- Widespread use of in-home care, senior living arrangements, and hospices.
- Increased investment in research for cancer, cardiovascular, and other age-related illnesses.
- Shortage of nurses, combined with increasing demand for their services, will necessitate better tools to get the job done.
- Increased organ donations, better organ-preservation and tissue-bank technology.

Increased Per Capita Income

Because of the shrinking family size, per capita income has risen to a level that is 50 to 100 percent higher than that of the U.S. There will be an increased interest in ever more sophisticated gadgetry and extravagant amenities. Japan is already leading the way in all sorts of home appliances, such as HDTV, and is primed for the next gadget—maybe the Internet television. Japanese will be looking for more exotic vacation spots and more families to be traveling together, as opposed to traditional large package-tour groups. "Slow Life" is a term for people who are hoping take it easy and spend more time on leisure activities. "My Car Life" indicates a trend toward the luxury lifestyle that car ownership implies in a crowded country.

Changes in the Banking and Financial Industry

This will have a long-term impact on how people use their money. Japanese have gradually been moving away from their traditional approach of saving a high percentage of disposable income at very low interest to investing in the stock market and even overseas. For example, the Japanese version of the individual 401(k)-type of retirement investment scheme, which started in May of 2000, has shot up to create a huge market for individual investment. In the year 2007, for the first time ever, new private investment surpassed new corporate investment. Foreign banks have entered the Japan market, setting trends in service and innovation. Major banks have entered into heretofore unheard-of mergers. Thanks to an aggressive push by then-PM Koizumi, even the all-mighty Postal Bank of Japan has evolved into the semiprivate Japan Post, and is the largest bank in the world in terms of individual deposits.

More Goods for Fewer Kids

The latest census projections indicate that the population may have already peaked several ahead of schedule at about 128 million, and possibly begun to decline. The Japanese census last year revealed that the population, at the current birthrate, will drop to around 107 million by the year 2050. The number of households without children has already risen from 40 percent to over 72 percent in the last forty years. With fewer babies being born, products specifically designed for kids are becoming more sophisticated and more expensive. Toy maker Bandai even came out with a 1.5-meter model robot based on the *anime* character Gundam that started at around ¥350,000 (US$3,200).

More Goods for More Spoiled Pets

Japanese dote on their pets and spare no expense. Pet clothing and special foods already command a premium. Pet grooming, veterinarian services, and obedience training are already on the rise. On-line services for pets are a booming business. On a recent visit to the Ginza we spotted a dog fully dressed in a child's dress, complete with sun bonnet, in its own baby stroller.

Factoid

In 1999, Japan changed the official definition of death from the heart not beating to brain death. This allowed for human organs to be legally transplanted for the first time.

Uniquely Japanese Version of the Internet Economy

Japanese consumers, who already have famously high standards, will continue to become even more sophisticated and demanding. Access of the Internet via wireless devices is exploding. Many people have more than one cell phone and treat them as must-have accessories rather than tools. The range of cell phone accessories is amazing—ever thought about dressing yours in a tiny kimono or biker jacket? While the current main Internet use on the cell phone is e-mail text messaging, other uses have already taken off: Internet browsing and entertainment functions, video phones, video games, TV shows and movies, downloadable books, etc. Next will be home networking devices connecting all products within the home, while seamlessly connecting them with mobile products outside the home. There is a recognized shortage of basic parts, such as flash memory and LCDs, for these developments.

Increases in Internet Connectivity

Lowering of connectivity fees, combined with an emphasis on user friendliness, will open up Internet applications to much younger and much older audiences. Japanese pay almost the same monthly rates as in the U.S., but they get speeds up to twenty times faster. Wireless devices will increasingly help seniors get around, order goods and medicines, and get better in-home health care. Children will find more exciting games and better remote-learning materials. Parents now have a range of tracking devices for their kids' safety. Schools, such as the infamous cram schools, are starting to go online. Internet interface devices and individual entertainment and learning systems that include video and audio and that can be worn and used while riding the trains will be developed. Also, business-to-business applications will explode, as companies enjoy the efficiencies to be gained from streamlined ordering, purchasing, and delivery processes. The fulfillment industry, already geared for just-in-time inventory systems, will see further jumps in efficiency.

More Internationally Known Sports Stars and Actors

The Ichiro phenomenon (and now Matsui, etc.) has demonstrated Japan's potential to make it to the top in international professional sports, giving young people greater inspiration to pursue their athletic dreams and purchase the latest gear. Not just Japanese but many other Asians look to these Japanese players in the U.S. as a source of pride. They are happy to keep up with the U.S. Major League games and purchase the paraphernalia associated with their hero. A few breakthrough Japanese actors and actresses have made the Hollywood scene—as either their English improves or the general receptivity for Japanese-language films increases.

More Japanese Travelers Farther Afield

Rather than limit foreign travel to the stereotypical tourist destinations, Japanese are already charting new itineraries. There are already package tours for viewing the Aurora Borealis in Alaska or the Galapagos Islands off the coast of South America. One of fallen entrepreneur Takafumi Horie's unrealized schemes included a plan for a space-tourism business.

Higher Divorce Rate

In 1970 there were over one million marriages and only 96,000 divorces. By 2004, the marriage rate had fallen to 720,249, while the divorce rate had jumped to 270,815 (*Japan Almanac*, 2006). Both marriage and divorce are happening later in life in Japan. This rising incidence of separations will no doubt mean an increase in household care services especially aimed at single seniors and in job-placement and career-development services, especially for women. As an example, a few laid-off salary men have been enterprising enough to go into the house-cleaning business, which would have been unheard of until the last few years.

Brand X or Brand Exclusive

In our previous book, we declared that bargain hunting in outlet stores and online, name brands removed, was already gathering force and that we could expect more value-consciousness for Japanese consumers. We were half wrong about this one. While real-estate prices dipped, the luxury-goods stores bought up prime real estate in the best spots in Ginza and Shibuya. Now that the economy is bouncing back, so are the luxury-goods shoppers, who now have the range of options from no-brand to the always-popular Burberry to BMW and beyond! And we can expect to see more of the famous brands moving in as the baby boomers retire.

Other Predictions for Japan

In addition to the above predictions, our observations, conversations, and gut feelings are telling us that the following could occur over the next decade:

- More mental health care and perhaps a model that will be exported to other parts of Asia. More prescriptions by physicians for antidepressant, anticonvulsive symptoms. Many of these prescriptions are already being approved by the Ministry of Health, Welfare, and Labor.
- Exporting sake and beer around the world.
- More college-aged kids studying abroad, more

foreign students in Japan (especially from China).

- More immigrants from other countries. Could it possibly be a crack in the *shoji* (paper sliding doors)?

- Healthcare—less convenient to smoke and more people working out at gyms, doing yoga, etc. "Healthy living" stores abound (organic stores, Natural Lawson).

- More international travel, especially among the silver generation.

- More interest in studying in science and technology in Japan—most likely by other Asians. Japan has ten universities ranking in the top two hundred around the world, and the most technologically advanced companies on the planet.

This section has no doubt given you some interesting ideas about what's going on in Japan now, and what might be coming along in the future. Japan has a lot to offer—and the market will only get more sophisticated. Japanese have the means to be about the most discerning consumers on the planet—it's a matter of having something that will appeal to their tastes and high standards. Working with a Japanese partner on the development of new products could be your key to success in the rest of Asia as well. You don't have to take our word for it. Go to Japan, take a good look around and see for yourself. Perhaps you have some predictions to share with us—we welcome that. Our contact information is at the back of the book in the Epilogue. The next chapter on "Beyond Survival" might give you some hints about some of our favorite places to visit beyond your hotel, factory, or office.

CHAPTER 7

Beyond Survival: Exploring Japan

Business interactions in Japan proceed well in direct proportion to one's familiarity with the terrain, the people, and the arts, and culture. Indeed, the sights and customs of Japan hold such enormous appeal that it would be wasting a valuable opportunity not to experience some of them while there on business. The information and insights gained by doing so can enhance substantially the all-important effort to build and maintain relationships with Japanese counterparts and customers.

Learning from Your Surroundings

Take an analytical approach when you go traveling in Japan: you can learn a lot about the country by visiting a few key places and making astute observations. The spectrum of your visits might include the following:

- Some well-known tourist spots (see our suggestions in this chapter)
- Convenience store (statistically, there should be one within a five minute walk from where you are now)
- Gas station
- Supermarket
- Major train or subway station, especially at rush hour
- Buddhist temple or Shinto shrine
- Art, historical, or other cultural museum
- Department store, including basement and top floors
- Electronics shop
- Traditional Japanese crafts maker (harder to find)
- School (you will need an escort to get in)
- Factory or assembly site
- Drinking establishment, including a traditional coffee shop
- Local noodle stand
- Hospital (especially if your industry is medically related)
- Drug store
- Bookstore

If free time is very limited, you can still get out of your hotel room, walk down the street, and find the nearest convenience store, temple or shrine, subway station, or any place of business. Even observations of goings on in the hotel lobby can be a rich source of learning.

What to Observe

Take on the role of business and cultural detective and note both the obvious and subtle differences: How are things organized? How do people behave? What is the level of customer service? How are goods displayed? How do people buy and pay for goods and services? How do people work together and communicate? How do people greet each other? Is there an obvious hierarchy? What are people reading? What attracts attention and what is avoided?

Spirituality

To know a country, one needs to know its religions. Fortunately, Japan is a place where some of the most scenic spots also happen to be religious sites—Buddhist temples and Shinto shrines—that are very worth seeing.

Sightseeing in Japan

In Tokyo

Meiji Shrine Meiji Shrine was the place of worship for the Emperor Meiji, and the scale of this shrine and its 178 acres of grounds and surrounding park in the heart of downtown Tokyo are a tribute to the royal connections. The promenade through which one enters the enormous *torii* gate gives a feeling of royal splendor. Enjoy the Japanese garden, particularly in the summer months when the thousands of irises are in full bloom. Nearing the shrine, one can purchase a prayer slate on which to write a wish. Standing in front of the shrine, visitors toss a coin into the offering box, clap their hands twice, and offer a prayer—usually in hopes of good fortune in a specific area of life.

Harajuku Right next to Meiji Shrine, in Harajuku, one finds a total contrast of old to new in the hundreds of modern boutiques, trendy restaurants, and hip youth preening in the latest fashions. This is the place to see what's the latest in Japan. Check out the store across the street from the station, usually devoted to whatever the current trend is, and probably something cute—cute is always "in" in Japan.

Roppongi Hills and Tokyo Midtown See how Japan is moving upscale—*way* upscale. An overwhelming panoply of state-of-the-art designer clothing and accessory stores, restaurants, business facilities, a five-star hotel with suites going for US$20,000 a night, all within these two many-story, gorgeously appointed architectural wonders. What we want to know is how did Starbucks manage to snag that prime corner location at the ground floor entrance? Success happens, even to non-Japanese businesses in Japan.

Shibuya The birthplace of Japan's Bit Valley is as much concept as place, but Shibuya is well worth a visit to see the bustle of Internet-related activity and to experience the trendy shopping, cafes, and nightspots. You cannot miss the wide array of fashion and hairstyles.

Chinzanso For those wishing to experience a beautiful, elegant Japanese garden within the confines of Tokyo, Chinzanso is the place. Located adjacent to the Four Seasons Hotel, Chinzanso features the entire repertoire of a traditional Japanese garden and more. One finds ponds, a watermill, large pagoda, a shrine, waterfall tunnel, garden sculptures, as well as beautifully manicured pines and other shrubs. The path in the garden is quite manageable. In summer months, the garden is lit up with hundreds of small lights representing fireflies which in bygone days were transported live from rural Japan to the garden every year.

Asakusa The best of old Edo. This is where one finds a huge red lantern hanging under the temple gate, the entrance to Asakusa Kannon temple. Along the grand mall leading to the temple, one finds all sorts of traditional Japanese handicrafts, baubles, and treats. The scent of incense wafts through the air. One can purchase a stick of incense and place it in the prominent sacred incense burner at the front of the temple, for good fortune.

The Ginza Japan's answer to New York City's Fifth Avenue or the Champs-Élysées in Paris—pricey, with eye-catching displays on all sides and high-class restaurants. Louis Vuitton has its largest store here. No evidence of economic downturn in sight. Bars can be quite pricey too; many are for members only. The elaborate neon displays of Ginza are well worth an evening stroll.

Shinjuku One of the newer areas of Tokyo, Shinjuku has much to offer in the way of first-class hotels, restaurants, nightlife, and a shop-till-you-drop atmosphere. The architecture on the west side of Shinjuku Station is distinctive; the buildings there are the tallest in the city because the land is bedrock, rare in earthquake-prone Tokyo. Kinokuniya Bookstore, with branches at both the east and south exits, has perhaps the best selection of English-language books in Japan.

Akihabara For the gadget aficionados, this is the best place to experience state-of-the-art Japanese electronics. There are hundreds of stores and shops in a dynamic environment of nonstop sound and flashing colors. For real bargains, try the duty-free floors of the larger stores. On our most recent trip to Japan, it seemed that the once-predominant aisles of still cameras, videocams, mini-TVs, PDAs, and cell phones had all but merged into a one-section display of uber-mobile phones/handheld devices, which does all of the above.

Ueno Famous for its park, museums, and zoo. A great place to come for outdoor stalls, featuring everything from shoes to dried squid to pineapple on a stick. Ueno Park is large and offers a pleasant stroll among large green trees.

Tsukiji Fish Market If you want to see up close one of the reasons Japan maintains its sushi superiority, and you happen to be up at 4 a.m. in Tokyo due to jet lag, the Tsukiji fish market is absolutely the place to go. How they track, analyze, price, and bid on the fish from dock to delivery holds all the thrill of watching a high-paced action movie unfold.

Near Tokyo

Yokohama Check out the largest Ferris Wheel in Japan and Yokohama's famous China Town. Good food is to be had anywhere. It's invigorating to stroll down to the waterfront and take in the never-ending traffic of shipping activity in this port that doesn't sleep.

Kamakura A favorite day trip from Tokyo, Kamakura offers more charm and ambience than just about any other city near Tokyo. The town, a haven for artists, is symbolized by its large outdoor statue of Buddha that is often seen in pictures of Japan. One look can give you that feeling of "This is why I came to Japan." There are dozens of temples—many of which have beautiful seasonal floral displays—and shrines tucked away in the gentle hills in this town. There are many delightful shops overflowing with local crafts, and tiny but alluring eating establishments.

Nikko Especially beautiful in the fall, Nikko features an amazing intensity of autumn color (due to the tiny size of the Japanese maple leaf). The Toshogu Mausoleum is an excellent example of rococo architecture in Japan. Within the elaborate carvings one finds the celebrated three monkeys who signify "Hear no evil, speak no evil, see no evil." Nearby, check out Kegon Falls, one of Japan's finest waterfalls. In winter, the water freezes, creating a startling visual delight likened to an oversized icicle.

Hakone On a clear day, you can look out over Lake Ashinoko and see a picture-perfect Mount Fuji smiling at you, as on so many postcards. Hakone is famous for its many hot spring resorts and beautifully hand-crafted wood products.

Tokyo Disneyland Just kidding about this one. Actually it might be worth looking into if you have kids, or are interested in seeing one of the hottest dating spots in Japan. It is also Disney's highest-grossing property worldwide, and so popular they've added on Disney Sea. Added in 2001, it is unique in the world, and features attractions themed after Disney movies having to do with the Ocean.

Odaiba–Venus Forte This is the place where Japan meets Las Vegas meets Fifth Avenue meets Disney's version of Old Italia. Built on landfill in Tokyo Bay, Odaiba features hundreds of shops, restaurants, and other establishments. The Ferris Wheel here is the second largest in Japan. The Toyota showroom is so spacious that one can actually "test drive" a remote-controlled electric vehicle. There is an amusement park with nothing but virtual rides covering themes from mystery to Jurassic Park. This playground can be reached by its own special train, called "Yuri-ka-mome," from Shimbashi in about twenty minutes.

Central Japan

Nagoya Most people don't associate Nagoya with hot travel destinations, but since so much business is conducted in this central region, it's not unlikely that you'll find yourself with some time here. The Port of Nagoya offers an excellent boat tour via a very stylized goldfish-shaped boat. As Nagoya is among the busiest ports in the world, this makes for an economically insightful couple of hours. Meiji Mura (Meiji Village), where samurai dramas and period movies are filmed, offers its own small Japanese version of Universal Studios.

> **Factoid**
>
> Japanese spend over ¥150,000 (US$1,500) a year per capita on travel within Japan. While not cheap, Japan is one of the most convenient and safest countries for travel in the world, thanks to the extensive infrastructure of the travel industry. Trains and buses go everywhere, and one can find every sort of accommodation from Youth Hostels to fancy hotels to traditional Japanese inns (*ryokan*) to *tatami*-mat guest rooms in temples.

Hokkaido

Sapporo Capital of Japan's final frontier and home of the 1972 Winter Olympics, Sapporo is laid out like a grid (based on German city planning). The Sapporo Snow Festival boasts the most intricate snow and ice sculptures in the world. The landscape here, wide open and dotted with cattle ranches, is markedly different from the rest of Japan. A true delight is to have "Gengis Khan" (*jin-*

gisukan) all-you-can-eat Asian barbeque, while drinking world famous Sapporo Beer, if possible at the Sapporo Beer Hall.

Kansai Area

Osaka Home of Osaka Castle and traditional Japanese puppetry called Bunraku. Osaka features a unique restaurant district, Kuidaore, literally "eat till you drop"—and world-class entertainment. A famous regional culinary delight is *okonomiyaki*, a combination of pancake and omelet loaded with cabbage, other vegetables, and the meat or seafood of your choice. Universal Studios Osaka and the Osaka Aquarium provide fun family entertainment. Or you could be daring and visit Spa World to get a taste of the modern-day Japanese bath and spa. Don't miss putting your feet into the pool of hundreds of tiny fish who nibble at your toes. A sensation like no other!

Kyoto An ancient capital of Japan, Kyoto is also known as the country's cultural center. You can hardly say you've been to Japan if you haven't visited Kyoto. The city offers the best of old Japan in its temples, shrines, castles, and gardens. Must-visit sites include Ryoanji Temple with its famous rock garden, Temple of the Golden Pavilion, Silver Pavilion, Nijo Castle, Kiyomizu Temple, and the Imperial Palace grounds.

Nara An even more ancient capital, Nara features the world's largest wooden structure, a huge temple housing an enormous bronze-cast Buddha (*daibutsu*), even larger than the more famous outdoor Buddha at Kamakura. There is also the Horyuji, one of Japan's oldest Buddhist temples, just outside of Nara, with its incredibly beautiful architecture, sculpture, and painting.

Southwest of Osaka

Hiroshima Every world citizen should visit the Atomic Bomb Memorial Museum and the monument to the victims of nuclear destruction. It is an unforgettable experience.

Himeji The picturesque castle here is regarded as Japan's most impressive. It was used as the setting for many of Kurosawa's films, as well as the American television miniseries "Shogun."

Top Festivals in Japan

Almost every community in Japan stages one or more local festivals (*matsuri*) every year. Listed below are some of the major ones. Check with a local travel agency well in advance for transportation and accommodation. Japanguide.com is another a good source of useful travel and other information.

- Snow Festival, *Sapporo Yuki Matsuri* (Sapporo, February). World-famous snow and ice sculptures on display.
- Gion Festival, *Gion Matsuri* (Kyoto, July). Features special lanterns and a parade.
- Teijin Festival (Osaka, July). Numerous decorated boats on display with life-sized figurines and torches.
- Nebuta Festival (Aomori, August). Night parades featuring elaborate, illuminated papier mâché floats.
- Tanabata Festival (Sendai, August). While centered in Sendai, this festival is celebrated throughout Japan. Tall bamboo poles decorated with colored streamers.

- Seven-Five-Three, *shichi-go-san* (November, all over Japan) Celebration for children to dress in traditional Japanese wear and go to the local Shinto shrine for a blessing.

Other Seasonal Events

- Cherry blossom viewing, *hanami*, in early April. Usually includes raucous parties and plenty of sake and singing, which take place under the blizzard-like falling cherry blossoms.
- Summer fireworks festivals, *hanabi*, which occur in most parts of Japan throughout the summer.
- Autumnal leaf viewing, *momijigari*. Japan's fall season is truly gorgeous, rivaling the best of the U.S. Northeast, but with shrines, gardens, and castles as a backdrop.

Relaxing Japanese Style

- Take in a Japanese garden such as the one at Meiji Shrine, Chinzanso, or Shinjuku Gyoen.
- Stroll through the local shrine in the early evening.
- Check out a local festival—almost every week there's one going on somewhere.
- Attend a Japanese tea ceremony—an ancient ritual centered on the simple task of preparing tea for one or more guests. The experience can approach a zen-like quality. On entering the tearoom, one is immediately aware of the austere beauty of the interior, often with only a single scroll hanging above a single vase holding a solitary flower. The distractions of daily life are shut out. The mind focuses only on what is at

hand. The silence inside the room casts a meditative ambience, punctuated only by the sounds of hot water being scooped from the kettle to the tea bowl along with the orderly swishing of the bamboo whisk creating the frothy green tea.

After eating a small sweet, one is invited to drink the special tea from a ceramic bowl chosen especially for the occasion. Typically, host and guests sit on their knees on the *tatami* floor. Guests may sit in any way that is comfortable, so that one's legs don't fall asleep, which can happen if one is not accustomed to sitting in the *seiza* fashion (on your knees with feet tucked under the body). The large gardens on the premises of many major hotels actually contain special teahouses. These beautiful yet simple structures often have moss-covered stones leading to their entrances, along with delicate shrubs and textured bamboo fences.

Factoid

Japanese golfers have been known to pay hundreds of dollars for hole-in-one golf insurance. That's right. In this society of extreme mindfulness toward others, if someone gets a hole-in-one, he or she is expected to take the golfing group out for a fancy meal and sometimes even buy gifts for the entire work staff. Apparently a hole-in-one is considered bad luck, ergo the need to give lavish gifts to counter ill fortune. There have been cases of bankruptcy in the past, due to having too good a swing. We heard an interesting story of a Japanese golfer who got a hole-in-one while playing alone, so the caddy nonchalantly walked over, took the ball out of the hole, and placed it on the ground nearby, stating, "This way is much better."

- Visit an *onsen*, a Japanese hot spring bath. The experience will likely change one's relaxation standards. In fact, company outings in Japan traditionally took place at *onsen*, where the relaxed, meditative nature of the communal bath blunts the edges of business stresses and interpersonal rivalries and can enhance teambuilding. If your Japanese colleagues invite you to a hot spring, here are some useful hints to follow . . .

Don't offend your host by immediately refusing to participate. If you must refuse, do so with proper expressions of gratitude for the kind invitation. Japanese have a deep, visceral attachment to their bath, or *ofuro*. When they are living overseas, it's often what they say that they miss the most about Japan.

Be sure to wash yourself thoroughly and rinse the soap off before entering the bath. This goes for the bath at the *onsen*, at a Japanese inn, and in private homes. In Japan, the tub is for soaking, not bathing. The water is to be shared, so it should always be kept clean. Nothing would be more off-putting to the Japanese than seeing you get straight into the water without soaping and rinsing off first. Japanese bathrooms are designed with a drain in the floor and usually a hand-held shower outside the tub so you can wash yourself and rinse off thoroughly before entering the tub. Then after your soak, when you exit the tub, you might want to wash yourself off one more time, just to be sure of a thorough cleansing.

A proper Japanese *onsen* will provide you with a small, rectangular-shaped towel, which you will find quite useful in several ways during the bathing adventure. It's about the right size to cover your body's vital parts when you go from the changing room into the bathing area. You can also use it for soaping up and scrubbing your body. Rinse it off thoroughly and use it to drape over yourself on your way to the tub, then leave it outside the tub while you're in the water. When you exit the tub, drape it over yourself again on the way out. If a large towel is not provided, simply wring out this small towel and use it to dry off before dressing.

As some of our U.S. associates found out on recent trips to Japan, proper *onsen* etiquette also means many of them don't allow kids or tattoos. Calling in advance to check would definitely be advisable. In Japan, tattoos have a historical association with the criminal element of Japan, and it seems to be where hot spring proprietors draw the line.

Perhaps More Educational than Relaxing

Golf

As mentioned in Chapter 3, this can be an all-day event, used frequently to develop business relationships. Most golf courses in Japan are for members only. Individuals and companies have paid tens or even hundreds of thousands of dollars for the privilege of membership. Tee-times are taken very seriously, given the high demand, and generally have to be made in advance. The front nine might be played in the morning and the back nine in the afternoon, separated by a rather full lunch. It's important not to show up the senior person in your group, unless everyone knows you to be an expert golfer.

Guided Tours

These can be wonderful for seeing a lot of the area in an efficient manner, but in Japan there doesn't seem to be any such thing as a leisurely tour—you see at least twenty sites in one day, fifteen to twenty minutes at a site. It's a great way to get your bearings, though, and decide where you want to return later on. It's also a good way to see how Japanese present Japan to foreigners.

Shopping

The hustle and bustle and nonstop crowds can exhaust you almost before you start. However, if you'd like to experience the sort of commercial buzz which Japanese enjoy, go to any major department store and proceed to the *chika-ikkai* (first underground level) where you will find the food section. A number of different retailers are assembled there, selling everything from fresh *miso* (soy bean paste) to wines. Shouts of *"Irasshaimase!"* (Welcome!) or other phrases, which might be boasts about the taste of a particular item, contribute to the general cacophony. It's truly an experience for all five senses.

What to Bring Back from Japan?

Many of the following items can be found in the many gift stores at the extensive shopping malls of all the major international airports. Osaka's Kansai International Airport even has an entire department store adjacent to the airport.

- Watches: Lots to choose from, of high quality in any price range.
- Pens: Especially the multifunctional ones. Ito-ya is our favorite store with the best selections.

- Stationery goods: Some of the finest quality paper products in the world, fancy bookmarks, tiny staplers, interesting stickers and seals, wrapping paper, and gift bags.
- Business card holders (*meishi ire*)—the best of high-fashion designers are all represented.
- Gadgets: Japan is gadget heaven—just be sure that what you buy is electrically compatible with your outlets back home, and comes with a manual in your native language. Mini-disc CD recorders, video and still cameras, and MP3 players were all invented here. There's a raft of other stuff, along with complete fashion accessories for your iPod, mobile phone, etc. Check out the duty-free floors of the various large electronics stores in Akihabara, such as Llaox, Big Camera, Sakura, and others.
- *Yukata*: Light cotton kimono, which is available for purchase in virtually every hotel in Japan, and at traditional Japanese resorts is typically donned after the evening bath for a relaxing stroll during the hot summer months.
- Bridal kimono: Made of silk and elaborately embroidered. Not for the fiscally faint of heart—expect to pay over US$10,000 for a new one. Steep discounts are available for second-hand or rental kimono.
- Calendars: There are many with beautiful Japanese motifs.
- Lightweight, retractable umbrellas.
- Regional handcrafted items: Often found in specialty sections in department stores.
- Chopstick sets and holders.

- Unusual, specialized eating utensils, such as spoons that are just for eating strawberries and tiny forks that are just for eating cakes.
- Dolls: Popular varieties include the famous Hakata doll, the traditional, delicate, beautifully painted, usually kimono-clad doll that will delight collectors and kids equally; the *kokeshi* doll; or even Japanese Barbie Dolls or the more popular Rikka-chan.
- Handbags: Compact and full of compartments.
- Handkerchiefs and towels in any size and fabric, which may also depict local scenes.
- Scarves and mufflers: Bargains available, depending on the season.
- World-class pearls: Mikimoto, Tasaki, and others.
- Lacquer ware: Among the world's finest, with many regional variations. Trays, vases of all shapes, boxes, soup bowls, jewelry boxes, and more.
- Cloisonné wear, such as jewelry, framed art pieces, vases, lamp stands, and more.
- Ceramics, such as sake drinking sets and tea sets, and decorative bowls and plates.
- Japanese green tea or *ocha*: You can get it in vacuum-packed bags or the tea bag variety. Japanese also have their own selection of beautifully packaged black and herb teas.
- Unusual local food items: Beautifully wrapped or tinned snack foods, tasty cookies, candies, or even dried fish.
- Traditional woodblock prints and scroll paintings.

- *Furoshiki*: Beautiful square silk or rayon pieces for wrapping gifts and carrying special objects.
- Swords: Getting an authentic *katana* could turn into an all-day adventure. Only for true aficionados.

For the Kids at Home

- *Pokemon, Digimon, Yu-Gi-Oh!, Dragonball, Naruto,* and other *anime* cards, toys, and accessories.
- Traditional games: Origami, paper balloons, flat marbles.
- Small electronic toys and virtual pets (*Tamagotchi*) of any description from puppies to beetles.
- Toys: World's cutest stuffed animals found here, as well as toys for the bath.
- Sanrio character items: Hello Kitty, Kerroppi the frog, Spotty Dotty the puppy, Tare Panda, and the like.

CHAPTER 8

Useful Resources

Maps are a must for getting around in Japan, especially in the major cities. Particularly helpful are the Japan National Tourist Organization (JNTO) maps, which are bilingual and can be picked up free from any JNTO desk or office, or at their website: www.jnto.go.jp. Tourist information stands at major train stations will also have local maps.

Making Sense of a Japanese Address

Japanese addresses, unlike in most of the Western world, go from place to name—they start with Japan, then cite the prefecture, city, ward, block address, and finally the person's name. Named streets are rare and, in any case, generally not used in addresses. The buildings on any given block are numbered not in numeric sequence but in the order in which they were built. Good luck finding your destination!

TIP: If you don't have a map leading to your destination, ask for landmarks, nearby shop names, and the nearest train or subway station. Some companies include a map on the back of their business cards, to make it easier for prospective customers to find them. Even taxi drivers might need a map. They also carry several road atlases to help them maneuver, especially in places like Tokyo and Osaka. One begins to understand why car navigation systems were an instant hit in Japan and far outpace any other country in terms of sophistication and detail.

Not surprisingly, when Japanese plan to meet each other, they generally pick a well-known landmark or train station exit, rather than meeting at a particular place of business or private residence.

Brief Hotel Review

Tokyo

- **Akasaka Prince:** Sleek and elegant; good train connections.
- **ANA (All Nippon Airways):** Best hotel in the Roppongi area, fairly spacious rooms, beautiful lobby—a good place to meet someone.
- **Century Hyatt Shinjuku:** Good for business; new subway stop.
- **Four Seasons:** Located at Chinzanso with its adjacent Japanese garden. Luxurious and expensive; slightly inconvenient location.

- **Imperial Hotel:** Convenient, centrally located, recently renovated. Good for those who want to be near Tokyo's financial center or jog the perimeter of the Imperial Palace. The business center is quite well equipped with technically competent staff.
- **New Otani:** Central location across the street from the Akasaka Prince, with an exquisite Japanese garden and good business rates.
- **Okura:** Built prior to the Tokyo Olympics (1964), still reflecting '60s chic, and still luxurious and expensive. Not close to train or subway stations.
- **Park Hyatt:** Located just west of Shinjuku station, perhaps Tokyo's most luxurious hotel; on a clear day, one can see Mount Fuji. The Club Room makes a great meeting space.
- **Royal Park:** Great health club and pool; located near T-CAT (Tokyo City Air Terminal). Excellent traditional Japanese restaurant looking into the garden.
- **Westin:** Located at Ebisu Garden Place. Gorgeous, luxurious, expensive.
- **Conrad Hotel:** (In Shiodome.) Hilton's premier Tokyo property boasting of the largest spa in Tokyo and panoramic views of the Hamarikyu garden, a former royal residence.

Yokohama

- **Shin-Yokohama Prince:** Convenient to the bullet train (*Shinkansen*) station; good for business. A beautiful landmark; high-rise building.
- **The Yokohama Landmark Hotel:** Located

on the upper floors of the tallest building in Yokohama, this is truly a first-class hotel.

Osaka

- **Osaka Prince:** Very conveniently located and well appointed.
- **Imperial:** Recently renovated. Good location, great views of the river, not as expensive as the Imperial in Tokyo.

Japanese Culture through Cinema

Before you embark on your trip, a good way to get a feel for Japanese culture is to watch Japanese films or films about Japan. Below are some of our recommendations.

Comedy

- *Shall We Dance?* (Original Japanese version, not U.S. remake): A delightful slice of life of Japan— a typical Japanese white-collar guy, looking for more in life, suddenly takes up social dancing.
- *Tampopo* (Japan): A story about the quest for making the perfect bowl of noodles. Offers good cultural insights into how Japanese eat.
- *The Funeral* (Japan): A typical family funeral, with many ironic and humorous twists.
- *A Taxing Woman* (Japan): A female tax collector outwits one of the richest mob criminals in Japan—excellent insights into the Japanese bureaucracy.
- *Lost in Translation* (USA): A glimpse of Japan through the eyes of two very unlikely American visitors, brilliantly directed by Sophia Coppola.

- *The Story of Hachiko* (Japan): A touching, true story about a loyal dog who waits patiently at the station for his master to come home, even years after his master has died of a stroke.
- *Mr. Baseball* (USA): Hilarious and slightly goofy U.S. film—U.S. baseball player (Tom Selleck) goes to join the Japanese pro leagues.

Drama/Historical

- *Letters from Iwo Jima* (USA): A look from Japan's point of view at the Battle for Iwo Jima, directed by Clint Eastwood staring an all-Japanese all-star cast.
- *The Last Samurai*: An historical piece on the transition from the Samurai Era to the modern industrial age, starring Tom Cruise and Ken Watanabe.
- Any film by Akira Kurosawa: For example, *Seven Samurai* (a classic), *Ran* (Japanese rendition of King Lear), *Kagemusha*.
- *The Longest Day*: Japanese movie about the last day of WWII. Top leaders make the decision to surrender; the making of the Emperor's surrender speech.
- Anything by animation genius Hayao Miyazaki, including *My Neighbor Totoro*, *Howl's Moving Castle*, *Spirited Away*, and *Kiki's Delivery Service*.

For Kids

- *Doraemon*, *Anpan Man*, and *Pokemon* animation movies (Japan).
- *Sesame Street—Big Bird Goes to Japan* (USA): Hollywood's version of Japan for kids.

Studying Up on Japan

Contact the consulate in your area (or the Japanese Embassy in Washington, D.C.), which will have an information desk or branch of JETRO (Japan External Trade Organization) that can provide information to help you do business in Japan. For U.S. citizens, both pre-departure and post-return, your local Japan-America Society, particularly the Japan Society of New York, is a good place for information and programs on Japan.

Learning Japanese

- Local language schools/language services organizations: Be sure they cover business Japanese—check the Internet for local providers.
- Continuing education programs of local colleges and universities.

Self-Study of Japanese Language

- *Japanese for Busy People*, book and tape (or CD) set published by Kodansha International.
- *Interactive Japanese: An Introductory Course*, with tapes, by T. Tomoda and B. May, published by Kodansha.
- *Genki: An Interactive Course in Elementary Japanese*, with CD, published by the Japan Times.
- *13 Secrets for Speaking Fluent Japanese*, by G. Murray, published by Kodansha.
- *Living Language*, with CD, published by Random House.

Other General References

- Travel DVD on Japan (available through your local library, video store, or travel bookstore).

- *Nikkei Weekly*: Weekly digest of the *Nikkei Shimbun*, business and economy.
- *The Economist*: Weekly in-depth wrap up of worldwide economic events.
- *Bloomberg*: Financial news.
- *International Herald Tribune*: International news every other day.
- *Culturegrams*: A four-page reference guide for any country, updated annually. Pdf files or printed copies available at www.culturegrams.com.

Helpful Organizations and Web Sites

For a phone listing of major embassies, chambers of commerce, emergency contacts, and travel-related organizations, see the Appendix on p. 254. Check your favorite search engines as these Web sites are subject to change.

- Tokyo English Life Line (TELL) (03-5774-0992): An excellent resource to call when you need information on just about anything in English. Most staff members have (limited) counseling training to handle emotional issues along with the more mundane.
- TELL Counseling Services (For Japanese call 03-3498-0232. For English call 03-3498-0231): Provides face-to-face counseling in English, Japanese, German, Hindi, and Spanish.
- KDDI (0057): English-language telephone directory.
- Japan External Trade Organization (www. jetro.org): Provides a range of trade-related information.
- Japan Times Online (www.japantimes.co.jp): News reports on Japan.

- Asahi Online (www.asahi.com/english/): One of Japan's major newspapers, general news reports are online in Enlgish.
- Japan Guide (www.japanguide.com): Useful information about all aspects of Japan, including travel.
- Trends in Japan (web-japan.org/trends/): Business and economy, lifestyles, products, fashion, science, and technology are among the trends covered here.
- Expat exchange and expat forum (www.expat-exchange.com): A clearinghouse for expatriates around the world. You can get information as well as contribute articles.
- Connecting Expats in Japan (www.japan.alloexpat.com): Another all-purpose resource for foreigners living in Japan.
- Japan Zone (www.japanzone.com): Japan travel guide. Information on Japan and Japanese pop culture.

Web Alerts for Global News

Add these to your online daily news digests.

- BBC World
- Google Alerts
- MSNBC

Epilogue

What does it mean to be poised and ready in the global economy? It happens time and again: Otherwise competent business people rush off to Japan or some other foreign destination, hoping to return with bags brimming with yen or euro, only to find out soon enough that their hopes are dashed. The main reason? They have made no particular culture-specific preparation or strategy.

What then are the globally successful companies doing? Over the past five years we have noticed a significant increase in the number of leading edge and Fortune 500 companies that have begun to require cultural competency development as part of their overall global business strategy.

The first step in your due diligence process is to read up on your target culture, just as you have been doing by picking up this book. We recommend taking it one step further—developing your global business competency via intercultural coaching and facilitation. The purpose of this type of competency-building effort is to explore, develop, and practice the skills and strategies, many of which are outlined in this book, so that they become part of one's business strategy and personal style. Think of it as your dry run for the international business trip you are taking to any country. Start thinking about your intercultural competency strategy as a professional development investment that will show an immediate payback and give you a competitive edge.

With the advent of technological advances in information transfer in a "flat" world, we entertain great hopes of doing business around the globe instantaneously and successfully. Yet, while today's marketplace spans the globe, the tapestry of local cultures, values, and ways of conducting commerce remains mostly intact. Global business success is in direct proportion to one's ability to understand that tapestry and interact on local terms. In the past decade we have watched world events, conflicts, and wars that have further emphasized this nagging divide between cultures. In this global climate, we cannot ignore the urgent need for all world citizens to reach a greater level of understanding and tolerance as we become more economically and environmentally interdependent.

Is Japan worth pursuing? It can be daunting, to be sure. Yet, it is still the second largest economy in the world, with the best-educated workforce, one of the highest rates of savings, and arguably the most sophisticated consumer market in the world, harboring huge benefits for those willing to do what is necessary to penetrate the market. Japanese might consider it a pain in the neck to work with *gaijin* (foreigners), but the pain subsides and can even disappear in the measure that foreigners are open to doing their business in the Japanese way. That means consistent presence over a long period of time, novel technology, unassailable quality, trendy items, and an unfailing sense of customer service. It's best not to approach the market with a second-tier product and an attitude that "We are cheaper." In fact, the effort to compete on price alone will be a lost cause. Always emphasize quality and features, and by all means, deliver on what you promise.

The market is huge, per capita spending is very attractive, and Japanese consumers are sophisticated trendsetters. Japan is one of the most internationally experienced and politically stable countries in the world to do business. If you succeed in Japan, the returns will certainly make it well worth the effort and investment. Absolutely, Japan needs to be part of your global strategy. And now that you have your own personal business passport to Japan, our hope is that you will find your experiences there all the more rewarding and enriching. If you succeed in Japan, it won't be just the margins that will make the effort well worth the trouble and investment; you also will have passed the litmus test for success in the whole of Asia, and possibly the rest of the world as well.

Good luck with your Japan endeavors, or, as you will no doubt hear in Japan:

Gambarimasho!

(Good luck and let's go for it!)

Map of Japan

JR line

Shinkansen

HOKKAIDO

Sapporo

Kushiro

Hakodate

Aomori

Akita

Tohoku

Morioka

Yamagata

Sendai

Niigata

HONSHU

Kanto

Nagano

Chubu

Nagoya

Tokyo

Hiroshima

Kyoto

Chugoku

Fukuoka

Kinki
(Kansai)

Nara

SHIKOKU

Osaka

KYUSHU

Matsuyama

Nagasaki

Kagoshima

Naha

Okinawa

Around Tokyo

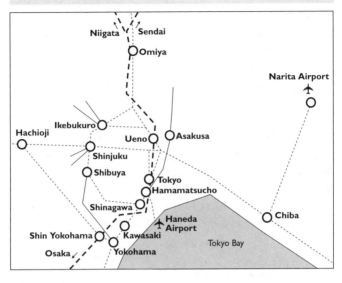

Around Osaka

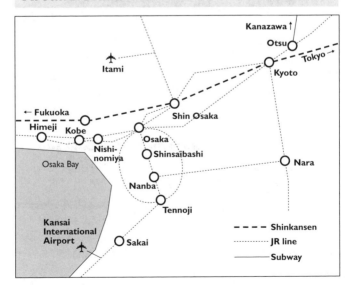

Useful Agencies and Numbers

Organization	Tel Number
Unites States Embassy	(03) 3224-5000
British Embassy	(03) 5211-1100
Embassy of France	(03) 5420-8800
Embassy of the Federal Rebulic of Germany	(03) 3473-0151
Embassy of Canada	(03) 5412-6200
Embassy of Spain	(03) 3583-8531
Embassy of the United States of Mexico	(03) 3581-1131
Embassy of the Federal Republic of Brazil	(03) 3404-5211
Amercian Chamber of Commerce	(03) 3433-5381
British Chamber of Commerce in Japan	(03) 3267-1901
Aultralian & New Zealand Chamber of Commerce in Japan	(03) 5214-0710
Korean Chamber of Commerce & Industry in Japan	(03) 3456-1190
German Chamber of Commerce & Industry in Japan	(03) 5276-9811

Numbers to Call for Emergencies

Police	110
Fire/Ambulance	119
Police in English	(03) 3501-0110
Hospital Information	(03) 3212-2323
The Japan Helpline	0120-461-977
Tokyo English Life Line	(03) 5774-0997

Travel and Tourist Information in English

Tourist Information	(03) 3201-3331
Travel Information	
Tokyo	(03) 3503-1461
Kyoto	(07) 5371-5649
Osaka	(06) 305-3311
Teletourist Service	(03) 3503-2911

Japan Rail East/West	(03) 3423-0111
Airport Flight Information	
New Tokyo International	(04) 7634-5000
Haneda	(03) 5757-8111
Osaka	(06) 856-6781
Kansai International	(07) 2455-2500
Japan National Tourist Organization	www.jnto.go.jp

Note: The country code for Japan is 81.

Japanese Holidays

January 1	New Year's Day
January 15	Coming-of-Age Day
February 11	National Foundation Day
March 21	Vernal Equinox
April 29	Greenery Day
May 3	Constitution Memorial Day
September 15	Respect-for-the-Aged Day
September 23	Autumnal Equinox
October 10	Health-Sports Day
November 3	Culture Day
November 23	Labor Thanksgiving Day
December 23	Emperor's Birthday

Notes on Holidays: The three holidays that fall between April 29 and May 5 have come to be known as Golden Week. Many Japanese take the entire week off, and many businesses slow down or close during that time. The same is true of the days just before and after New Year's Day (Oshogatsu). The season known as Obon (celebrated in mid-July in some parts of Japan and mid-August in others), while not an official national holiday, amounts to a widespread unofficial one. Many people take a few days off to return to their hometowns to reconnect with their families and pay respects to the spirits of departed family members.

It's best to avoid these three major holiday seasons for doing business. But if you must be in Japan during or close to these time frames, be sure to check with your Japanese business colleagues and customers as to their availability and secure reservations well in advance.

Bibliography

American Chamber of Commerce in Japan, The. *Setting Up an Office in Japan*. Tokyo: Charles E. Tuttle Co., 1994.

Asahi Shimbun. *Japan Almanac 2006*. Tokyo: Asahi Shimbun Publishing Company, 2005.

Bix, Herbert P. *Hirohito and the Making of Modern Japan*. New York: HarperCollins Publishers, 2000.

Brannen, Christalyn, and Tracey Wilen. *Doing Business with Japanese Men: A Women's Handbook*. Berkeley, CA: Stone Bridge Press, 1993.

Brigham Young Kennedy Center. *Culturegram 2001: Japan*. Provo, UT: Brigham Young University Press, 1999.

Clarke, Clifford G., and Douglas Lipp. *Danger and Opportunity: Resolving Conflict in U.S.-Based Subsidiaries*. Yarmouth, ME: Intercultural Press Inc., 1998.

Collins, Robert J. *Japan-Think, Ameri-Think: An Irreverant Guide to Understanding the Cultural Differences Between Us*. New York: Penguin Books, 1992.

Condon, John C. *With Respect to the Japanese*. Yarmouth, ME: Intercultural Press, Inc., 1984.

De Mente, Boyé Lafayette. *The Japanese Have a Word for It: The Complete Guide to Japanese Thought and Culture*. Chicago: Passport Books, 1997.

Economist, The. *Pocket World in Figures 2000*. London: Profile Books, Ltd., 1999.

Engle, Dean, and Ken Murakami. *Passport Japan: Your Pocket Guide to Japanese Business, Customs, and Etiquette*. Novato, CA: World Trade Press, 2000.

Farrell, William R. *Opportunity and Crisis in a Changing Japan*. Westport, CT: Quorum Books, 1999.

Friedman, Thomas L. *The World is Flat: A Brief History of the Twenty-first Century*. New York: Farrar, Straus and Giroux, 2005.

Holroyd, Carin, and Ken Coates. *Success Secrets to Maximize Business in Japan: A Hands-On Guide to Tackling Japanese Business Culture*. Culture Shock! Success Secrets to Maximize Business. Portland, OR: Graphic Arts Center Publishing Company, 1999.

Itasaka, Gen. *100 Tough Questions for Japan*. Kodansha Bilingual Books (English and Japanese). Tokyo: Kodansha International, 2006.

Japan External Trade Organization. *Nippon 2000: Business Facts and Figures* (Bilingual, English and Japanese). Tokyo: Japan External Trade Organization, 2000.

Kodansha International. *Talking About Japan Q and A*. 3rd ed. (Kodansha Bilingual Books.) Tokyo: Kodansha International, 2000.

Kohama, Masayuki. *Nine Hints for International Business Success* (Japanese language only). Tokyo: Mainichi Shimbun, 2000.

Kuroyanagi, Tetsuko. *Totto-chan: The Little Girl at the Window*. Translated by Dorothy Britton. Tokyo: Kodansha International, 1981.

Lewis, Richard D. *When Cultures Collide: Leading Across Cultures*. London: Nicholas Brealey Publishing Ltd., 1996.

Magee, David. *Turnaround: How Carlos Ghosn Rescued Nissan*. New York: HarperCollins Publishers, 2003.

McAlinn, Gerald Paul. *The Business Guide to Japan*. Business Guide to Asia. Singapore: Reed Academic Publishing Asia, 1996.

Meyer, Milton W. *Japan: A Concise History*. Totowa, NJ: Littlefield, Adams and Company, 1976.

Morton, W. Scott, and J. Kenneth Olenik. *Japan: Its History and Culture*. 4th ed. New York: McGray Hill, 2005.

Murtagh, Niall. *The Blue-Eyed Salaryman*. London: Profile Books, Ltd., 2006.

Nippon Steel Corporation. *Nippon: The Land and Its People*. Tokyo: Nippon Steel Corporation Human Resources Department, 1999.

Nishiyama, Kasuo. *Doing Business with Japan: Successful Strategies for Intercultural Communication*. Honolulu: University of Hawaii Press, 2000.

PHP Institute, Inc. *Japan: A Business Traveler's Handbook*. Tokyo: PHP Institute, Inc., 1997.

Pyle, Kenneth B. *Japan Rising: The Resurgence of Japanese Power and Purpose*. New York: Perseus Book Group, 2007.

Rowland, Diana. *Japanese Business Etiquette: A Practical Guide to Success with the Japanese*. New York: Warner Books, 1993.

Shelley, Rex. *Culture Shock! Japan: A Guide to Customs and Etiquette*. Portland, OR: Graphic Arts Center Publishing Company, 1998.

Trompenaars, Fons, and Charles Hampden-Turner. *Riding the Waves of Culture: Understanding Diversity in Global Business*. 2nd ed. New York: McGraw Hill, 1998.

Index

Notes

About the Authors

SUE SHINOMIYA (formerly Kallenbach), president of Business Passport, is a business consultant, corporate trainer, coach, webinar leader, and entrepreneur specializing in global business effectiveness for international corporations, transferees, and global virtual teams. Sue holds an MBA from San Francisco State University, including a scholarship at the Institute of International Studies and Trade in Japan. Her nearly twenty-five years in the intercultural field have included nine years working and living in Japan, and nearly six years managing an on-site program at Intel, Japan. Hewlett Packard, Intel, The Gap, Nike, Tektronix, Procter & Gamble, and Starbucks number among her many clients. Sue is a Board Member of SIETAR USA, part of a worldwide professional intercultural network, and is a certified Global Diversity Workforce Practitioner.

BRIAN SZEPKOUSKI is president of Szepko International Inc., a consulting firm whose mission is developing individual and organizational effectiveness. He provides expertise in cross-cultural communications, international executive development, and strategic planning for global business expansion. In addition to training and consulting, he is a certified executive and life coach focusing on long-term excellence in global leadership. He has an MA in Human Resource Development and has worked as a PR executive for both Japanese and American corporations, including Tiffany & Co. Brian lived in Japan six years, studying at both Waseda University and Tokyo University Graduate School as a Rotary Ambassadorial scholar, and teaching English at a private high school in northern Japan.

China for Businesswomen

A Strategic Guide to Travel, Negotiating, and Cultural Differences

TRACEY WILEN-DAUGENTI

More and more Western businesswomen are working in and traveling to China. Based on interviews with women executives and entrepreneurs who have succeeded in China, this book offers straightforward advice for avoiding gender and cultural obstacles. Topics include travel, cultural awareness, credibility, negotiation protocol and process, harassment, and entertaining, plus background on women in Chinese history and society. Dr. Tracey Wilen-Daugenti is an executive in Silicon Valley and a frequent guest on local and national business media.

184 pp, 6 x 9", paper, ISBN 978-1-933330-28-0, $16.95

The Little Tokyo Subway Guidebook

Everything You Need to Know to Get Around the City and Beyond

IBC PUBLISHING

Prepared with the official cooperation of the Tokyo Metropolitan Bureau of Transportation and Tokyo Metro Co., Ltd., this little guidebook has everything you need to negotiate Tokyo's vast subway system with confidence. Includes maps with color-coded details on all thirteen subway lines, information on ticketing, tourist fares, and commuter passes, helpful phrases, Exit Finder, and much more! An excellent pre-travel purchase for planning your trip and your voyage from the airport to downtown.

96 pp, 4¼ x 5⅞", paper, ISBN 978-4-896844-57-3, $9.95

Doing Business with Japanese Men

A Woman's Handbook

CHRISTALYN BRANNEN AND
TRACEY WILEN

The only book to look at the *uniquely* delicate situation every Western businesswoman faces traveling to Japan or meeting Japanese clients at her home office. Using real-life anecdotes, cultural explanations, and extensive lists of tactics, it tells women how to quickly establish their authority and work effectively.

176 pp, 5½ x 8½", paper, ISBN 978-1-880656-04-4, $9.95